The Last Cod-Fish

Other titles in the same series :

A mess that deserves a big NO, by Pierre Elliott Trudeau
The Traitor and The Jew, by Esther Delisle
Nine Fateful Challenges for Canada, by Deborah Coyne
Zen and the Art of a Postmodern Canada, by Stephen Schecter

By the same author :
The Living Ice, McClelland & Stewart, 1980

Canadian Cataloguing in Publication Data

Chantraine, Pol, 1944-
    The last cod-fish : life and death of the Newfoundland way of life
    (Food for thought ; 1)

    ISBN 1-895854-00-8 (0-921692-45-5 for Newfoundland)

    1. Fishery conservation - Grand Banks of Newfoundland. 2 Fishery manage-
ment, International - Grand Banks of Newfoundland. 3. Fishery resources -
Grand Banks of Newfoundland. 4. Cod - Fisheries - Grand Banks of Newfoundland. I. Title. II. Series : Food for thought (Montreal, Quebec) ; 1.

SH229.C4213 1993   639.9'770916344   C93-096289-3

If you wish to receive our lists of forthcoming titles, or submit manuscripts
for publication, please send your request to the following address :
Robert Davies Publishing,
P.O.B. 702, Outremont, QC, Canada H2V 4N6

Pol Chantraine

The Last Cod-Fish

Life and Death of the
Newfoundland way of life

translated by Käthe Roth,
revised by the author

ROBERT DAVIES PUBLISHING
MONTREAL – TORONTO

DISTRIBUTED IN CANADA BY

Stewart House,
481 University Avenue, Suite 900
Toronto, Ontario M5G 2E9

☎ *(Ontario & Québec) 1-800-268-5707*
(rest of Canada) 1-800-268-5742
Fax 416-940-3642

Proofread by Vicky Ross

*In memory of the eight victims
of the sinking of the «Nadine»,
during the night of 16-17 December , 1990:*

Pierre CYR, *Engineer-in-second
Lauréat* DEVEAU, *Cook
Estelle* LABERGE, *Biologist
Mario* LEBLANC, *Chief engineer
Jacquelin* MIOUSSE, *Deck hand
Émile* POIRIER, *Deck hand
Augustin* VIGNEAU, *First mate
Gérard* VIGNEAU, *Deck hand*

*and for the two who were saved :
Robert* POIRIER, *Captain
Serge* POIRIER, *Bosun*

Newfoundland–Labrador and the Grand Banks

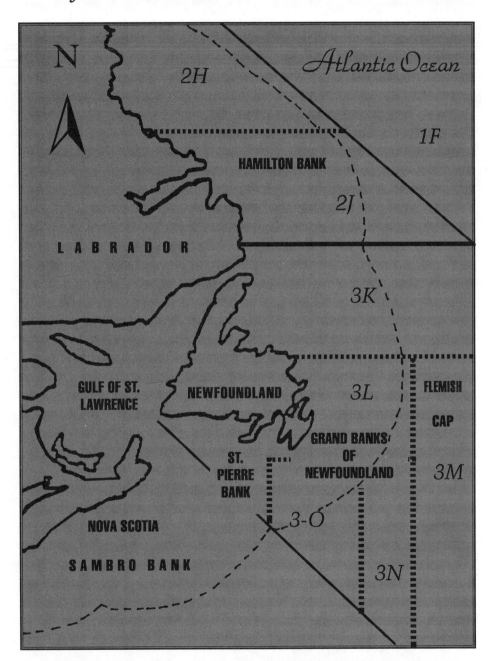

Map of Newfoundland-Labrador and the Grand Banks,
showing boundary divisions and sub-areas (hatched lines),
as well as the 200-mile fishing zone
over which Canada has sovereign jurisdiction

1

The Three Cod of Makkovik

BACK WHEN Ted Anderson started to fish, the cod came faithfully to Makkovik every year at the beginning of July. They swarmed in from the ocean in enormous schools, chasing the capelin that had come to spawn on the gravel beaches.

Ted is in his sixties now. His Norwegian and Innu ancestry has given him his high cheek-bones and prominent eyebrows, below which his deep-set eyes glow like embers. He has the powerful barrel chest of the aboriginals, the long legs of the Vikings, and there is a bounce to his step, like his Labrador forebears. In the brisk cold of late March in St. John's, Newfoundland, he goes bareheaded, his jacket unbuttoned, while passers-by, bundled in their warm parkas, shiver.

When he was young, Ted says, on a fine day—it was always a fine day when the last ice had released its hold on the shore and floated southward—the sea would begin to vibrate with capelin. Literally vibrate, alive with fish. Everywhere, as far as the eye could see, the water eddied and quivered, sparkled, turned almost effervescent as the little fish wriggled their dorsal fins.

This was the time for children to go down to the shore, from the head of the rock spit that dipped down into the ocean in the summer and was bordered with ice in the winter, where the family house was anchored against wind and time. There, with the water rising almost over the tops of their rubber boots, they filled buckets with the capelin crowding toward shore in the low swells in a state beyond excitement, a sort of unbridled sexual frenzy, the females to deposit their eggs in the gravel of the beach, the males to spray them with their milt. The water along the shore was thick and troubled.

By this time, the cod traps were already in the water. The men had checked the nets, mended the torn mesh, spliced the ropes, and solidly anchored the traps at sea, not too far from the shore. The box-shaped cod trap was made of net, weighted at the bottom and held up to the surface by floats, with a long net fence, or leader, extended across the flow of the tide. The fish that bumped into the leader swam along it through a vertical opening, or door, into the funnel-shaped trap, from which they could not escape.

The coastlines of Newfoundland and Labrador were sprinkled with these devices. In every outport, from Cape Race to northernmost Labrador—in the deep Bonavista, Trinity, Conception, and Notre-Dame bays, around every island left to the ocean as a souvenir by the Rock, with names like Fogo, Twillingate, Wabana, and Quirpon—fishing meant cod traps. Every morning that the waves were manageable, before the sun stained the horizon with glowing colours, the men went out in dories in teams of four or five, dipping their oars in the early days, later propelled by stuttering two-stroke engines, towing behind them a string of wide, open barges, which would hold the catch.

The fishermen dropped anchor at the cod trap and, with large long-sleeved dip-nets, began the tedious work of emptying it of the cod that had accumulated since the previous evening. In their oilskins, the traditional sou'westers clamped down on their heads, their cheeks swollen with fat quids of tobacco, they worked tirelessly, rocked by the swell to a state of drunkenness, hauling up the fish and throwing them, still squirming, into the barges. They stopped only to spit long streams of brown saliva into the ocean, which the wind sometimes spat back at their companions.

Ted Anderson remembers what it was like to get a gob smack in the face. From the right, ptui! In the time it took to turn and wipe it off with the sleeve of his oilskin, from the left, ptui! As a sort of self-defence, the young men getting salted in also began to chew tobacco; swats flew in all directions as the men dipped and drew the cod from the trap.

When the barges were full, the boats headed back to shore. With a flick of their knives, the men bled the cod, one by one, and passed them to others who, with a sure and expert grip, gutted them in a single pull. The livers were thrown into a barrel with one hand, while the other hand tossed the stomach and entrails to the gulls. With machine-like precision, the entire load was gutted. Then the cod were washed in the open water and packed into crates, which were hoisted to the top of high wharves, or "stages", to the salting bins. The head and dorsal bones were removed with a knife with a curiously twisted blade, the use of which was an art in itself, and the cod were ready for curing. A first layer was laid down, coarse salt was spread over it with a shovel, then another layer of fish, and so forth, until all the fish were preserved.

By now the sun was high in the sky and the fishermen stopped for lunch. Then they went back to the trap, took another load of fish, and gutted, beheaded, dressed, and salted them. And when this was done, if the cod were plentiful, there was yet a third trip to the trap late in the afternoon. Only when the sun stretched out the shadows on the ocean and turned the water amber and mauve, in the still hours when the wind held its breath for the evening calm and voices echoed against the cliffs, were the last crates of cod hoisted to the stages.

On good days, two and a half to three tons of cod were caught and salted, sometimes more. There were so many in the trap that one could walk on them. It was the same at Makkovik and Rigolet, at Cannaille Cove, Catalina, Aquaforte, Waddham, Bay d'Espoir, Fortune, Burgeo, and Argentia—in every marvellously named hamlet, village, and outport that formed a necklace around the Newfoundland and Labrador coasts notched with ancient fjords.

For three weeks without let-up, as long as the capelin were spawning on the coast, the men went out to the traps day after day. And when the capelin had finished their rites of reproduction, when the cod dispersed to the banks in search of other prey, the fishermen fished with the jigger, a hand-held line, with a lead-weighted three-pronged hook, that is dropped to the bottom, jerked up one or two fathoms (according to the fisherman's science), then lifted and plunged time and again, in measured, rhythmic movements, until a cod is hooked. There was such an abundance of fish that in one morning two men fishing this way could fill their dories. Depending on the nature of the fishing grounds and the fishermens' knowledge of the whereabouts of the fish, they might also use gill-nets and long lines.

This fishery lasted until late autumn in the southern bays. But in Makkovik, at 55° north latitude, fishing was just about over by mid-August. The men had fished by trap for three weeks, by jigger for three more, and they could certainly have gone on longer. But now, in the fine, sunny days of late summer, with their nights of already nipping cold, it was time to dry the cod. The fish were brought out of the brine, washed, and laid on long slatted tables (called flakes in New-foundland, *vigneaux* in the Gaspé, and *chaffauds* in Acadia) where they yielded up water, sweated off moisture, as they were turned now on the flesh side, now on the skin side, according to a predetermined sequence. After three days in the sun, they were stiff and had the texture of old leather; when flicked with a finger to determine their state of dessication, they sounded hollow. They could then be dry-packed and sent to the merchant, along with the barrels of cod-liver oil, the booty of the fishing season.

This is how northern cod were fished in northern Labrador. I chose to describe it through Ted Anderson's eyes because he and his generation, today in their sixties, are the last who knew the old way of life on the coast: an existence in harmony, symbiosis—almost synergy—with nature and the seasons. They were born and grew up there; they believed that they would make their living as had their fathers and grandfathers, and that their children would follow in their footsteps. But, just when they were reaching the prime of life, everything fell apart under their very noses. They noticed that the cod weren't filling their traps as they had in the past.

There were fewer fish every year. They quickly realized that it was the new ships, the big trawlers sweeping the bottom of the ocean with their nets, that were stealing their fish away.

When they protested, soothing statistics were served up to them, along with a dollop of various allowances, unemployment insurance, and so on. They were lectured on the ineluctable march of progress, the mysterious cycles of nature which alternated good years with bad—except that there were fewer and fewer good years. The fish were less abundant, and they were smaller. There were no more cod "as big as a man", the catches that had been the pride of the fisherman and in themselves ample compensation for a long day of labour. Many of the men were discouraged and moved to the cities; others took up new occupations. But those who remained in the tradition saw the unthinkable happen: in 1990, *only three cod were caught during the entire summer at Makkovik*, where once they had taken up to three tons every day!

The previous year (in September of 1989), at Tickle Black and Makkovik and along the entire Labrador coast, the cod were more plentiful than they had been in a long time. But this was their swan song! The nets of the inshore fishermen gave way under the load, and it took them an entire morning to gut and dress the catch before delivering it to the salting plant. Some thought that the times of plenty had returned. With joyful hearts, they rolled up their sleeves for their hard tasks; when they finished, they returned to sea to jig in the afternoon. The cod were a bit small, perhaps, the older men remarked, but it didn't matter when there were so many of them.

The news about the good fishing in Labrador soon spread along the coast and over to Newfoundland, and everywhere the fishing boats, seiners, longliners, and especially trawlers, large and small, set forth to fill their holds with cod.

At night, Ted Anderson told me, they could see the lights of the trawlers moving *en masse*, like a floating city, off Makkovik's shore. The enormous boats were gorging on fish, winching up and emptying their nets, then immediately shooting them back out into the water. The feast lasted almost two weeks, a real bonanza for everyone! Except for the inshore fishermen: they saw their catches plummet as the offshore fishing intensified, and they began to hate the large freezer-trawlers that scoured the ocean, over there, on the horizon, untouchable, and even ventured into coastal zones, ravaging nets and long lines while the fishing patrols slept.

In the end, something like six million pounds of cod were caught that year in Labrador waters, at Tickle Black and Makkovik. The entire fishing industry was jubilant. Only a few old men, prophets of doom, did not share in the general euphoria. Based on theories derived from their experience, they predicted dire times ahead. It was only in deference to their age that the brash young biologists, dripping with diplomas and armed with statistics, didn't laugh openly in their faces.

Except that the following year, the three miserable cod caught at Makkovik would prove the old men right. The super-trawlers, equipped with hyper-technology, had taken everything, right down to the last cod.

2

Dawn and Dusk of Labrador

THIS, THEN, WAS PROGRESS. This and the requisitioning of enormous areas of the game-stocked Labrador forest to create a training site for low-altitude NATO fighter jets. Labradorians of Ted Anderson's generation are not a little bitter when they take stock of the last thirty years. They feel that they were hoodwinked by mirages of prefabricated comfort while, behind the scenes, the way of life that made them happy was being destroyed.

Labradorians latched on to this unforgiving expanse of rock, far from everything, *at the end of the world*, as city people would say, without once suspecting that they represent another "end of the world", really a dead end of civilization. The ocean and the boreal forest stretching forever into the back country gave them everything they needed to live and, on top of that, the feeling of being in control of their lives, of being truly free. They were, and still are, people of nature, its children, somewhat outside the march of time.

When Ted Anderson's ancestor sailed from some Norwegian fjord and dropped anchor on this rugged coast more than a century ago, he didn't see, as others may have, a hostile Land of Cain. Labrador corresponded to certain ideas he had about the good life, with a taste of adventure and freedom. This life, the heritage of many generations of fishermen since the time of the Vikings, was, of course, inseparable from the sea and its fish. And the fish were *there*, as faithful as the seasons: abundant cod in the summer, salmon that came up the river to spawn in the gravel ponds far upstream, where the rock is steep and the clear water runs in resonant cascades, trout and char in the countless lakes. In the fall, great flights of fat, cackling geese stopped over in the marshes before starting their long voyage to their winter homes in Chesapeake Bay and Delaware. When they had left and the frost and snow squalls were trumpeting the return of winter, there were still huge herds of caribou to hunt in the forest, and traplines, springs, boxes, and other snares with which to harvest animals for furs. Nature was the provider of life.

Like many men who arrived in Labrador single, Anderson married an aboriginal woman. The story went that she was the prettiest in the village and was promised to the manager of the Hudson Bay trading post. But the Scandinavian curried her favour when her fiancé stayed away too long: the Hudson Bay man went to Montreal to trade furs, and by the time he thought about heading home the ice was already on the river, stopping all travel to Labrador. When he finally got back to his post the following spring, his winsome Innu had already married the immigrant Anderson, who had whisked her by dog-sled to Makkovik, far from the trading post and from any fits of jealousy.

On this spit of rock, caught between the ocean and the forest, the Andersons succeeded each other in the timelessness that belongs to people who live in balance with nature. Each generation, following in the footsteps of their forebears, found happiness and fulfillment. Knowledge and wisdom were transmitted from old to young through families and through communities that were homogeneous and tightly knit, as if to withstand the cold.

The rhythm of life followed a ritual orchestrated by time and weather: some things were done in their own good time and others when the season dictated. In July and early August, when the days were so long that the sun barely sank below the horizon at night, they fished for cod. This was the principal economic activity of the Labrador communities, and it brought in indispensable cash with which to purchase provisions in the south. The fishermen usually got little for their efforts: they were always swindled by the merchants, who paid them for their catch only just enough to sustain themselves to the following season when they would have to go at it again. But then, wasn't that the important thing, to keep on fishing?

With the money from the sale of their cod, they purchased winter provisions such as flour, molasses, bacon, lard, potatoes, turnips, and items they needed to repair their gear. They bought a few clothes as well, although furs were the most common material for clothing in northern Labrador up until the Second World War.

After that, the fishermen returned briefly to their fishing grounds to jig for the family's supply of cod for the winter. These fish, stuffed with capelin, were bigger, fatter, and, everyone felt, tastier.

Then it was time to store the lines and nets, since the season was tipping toward autumn: dusk was falling earlier and dawn came later. Already one's breath formed clouds in the air some mornings and there were thin skins of ice on the ponds. Snow squalls, pushed in by forbidding north winds, sometimes blocked out the afternoon light, underlining the urgency of the task at hand.

Saws and axes on their shoulders, the men harnessed up their teams of strong dogs and went out to cut their firewood. In September, the woods rang with the dry chop of hatchets and the whine of saws, while beside the forest paths grew stacks of logs that would feed fireplaces all winter long. They waited until the first snow made sliding easier before bringing back the formidable provisions needed to heat the little houses by the sea through the cold months. In the meantime, they used their time in the woods to scout the paths of small fur animals, for as soon as the cords of wood were laid in, it would be time for trapping. Fur is not a luxury in the high latitudes; it is life itself. When the temperature is forty or fifty degrees below zero Celsius, one's face quickly freezes without a fur fringe around the hood of one's parka.

October was the month for trapping, according to the seasonal round. While touring his traplines to see if the snares and his trickery had garnered his quota of animals, the trapper might shoot the occasional game bird or animal that showed its beak or snout. Wild geese, teals, hares, caribou—all were welcome in the cold cellar, to provide some variety from the salt cod and potatoes.

Come November, it was back to the sea yet again. From the labyrinth of channels, narrows, and straits of the vast Canadian arctic archipelago and the great bays that were being progressively swallowed by the ice-floes, hordes of Greenland seals were moving south. In a long, uninterrupted procession, they paraded for weeks by Makkovik and down the Labrador coast on their way to their winter home in the south. The ocean was alive with seals all the way to the horizon.

People in the village used solid rope nets to catch the pinnipeds. Their meat, cut into blocks, fed the sled dogs all winter long; their skin, tanned Innu style, was used to make boots and mittens.

The seals could not have chosen a better time to pass; soon Aeolus and his band would let loose their furious north winds, and braces of black clouds would dump blankets of snow over the naked Labrador coast. Already, the waves were breaking in great columns of foam on the reefs of the littoral, and the spray was building a dam of ice. The sea took on sombre, sinister colours; the sluggish swells hissed lugubriously and slowly covered it with a frozen shroud.

Now, with the maelstrom of winter roaring around them, the family gathered at the table in the glow of an oil lamp, in the sweet-smelling heat from the crackling wood fire, to listen to the cheerful reels, jigs, and fiddle tunes on the evening radio programmes from Rimouski. The contrast between the serenity inside the house and the throbbing, whistling, howling wind outside, its squalls lashing against the walls and shaking the foundation, gave full meaning to the work of the previous seasons. Here were the dividends for the endless days spent cod fishing, which had enabled them to fit the house out like a ship for the long voyage of winter; the salary earned on days passed among the blackflies in the woods, soaked with sweat, chopping enough wood to defy the bitterest cold; the interest paid on the game shot in the forest, the geese and ducks bagged in the marshes, and the fat seals taken in the nets to feed the dogs. . . .

Here was the true reward for this rough life, shared and negotiated with nature; no fortune or pot of gold could purchase the splendour of these moments of superb inner calm while the blizzards hammered the coast. This kind of happiness simply could not be bought, or transferred: one had to live one's entire life on the sea and in the woods to taste the full joy of these fleeting moments of abandon.

Ted Anderson told me, with a deep sigh, "That was life, my friend, true life!"

But time marched on. After Christmas and New Year, when winter had definitely settled in and the ice had gripped the countryside and the ocean in a yoke of blinding white, the Labradorians hitched up their dogs and left for the tracks of the tundra in search of animals to trap and game to shoot. On these expeditions in the cruel cold, which lasted many days, the men ran beside their sleds as much as they rode them, toiling for what were often meagre captures and scant pay when they delivered their furs to the Hudson Bay Company trading post. But these hunting trips were an integral part of life's ritual; without them, something would have been missing: the pact with nature would have been broken.

The pact would also have been broken if, in March, the men didn't feel a different fever, one that drew them back to the sea. There, among the chaos of the ice-floes and the gigantic icebergs shaken loose by the spasms of the arctic spring to drift and collide in the Labrador current, the Greenland seals, the same herd culled in the autumn for dog food had returned in the hundreds of thousands to pup on the ice.

Aside from marking a new turn in the seasonal cycle, the arrival of this bounty carried a sense of the imperative, for by now reserves were starting to decline. Also, the meals of salted fish and meat, the basic diet since winter began, were beginning to pall. The desire for fresh meat was pressing.

So the men went onto the ice to hunt the seal pups; the frenzy to renew their ties with the nurturing sea in this blood ceremony was so strong that almost no able man on the Labrador coast could resist it. It took them over, as if it were yet another rite, another devotion to nature, in which they proved themselves against the animals and the elements.

This was how March and April were spent. Then the seals left for the north, but in Makkovik people continued to eat seal meat, and only seal meat, until June, simply because there was nothing else. They waited for the return of the cod and they watched the ocean for the first ripples on the waves, announcing the mating dances of the capelin.

Today, without the cod, with a ban on seal hunting, and with a plan to increase the frequency of flights of low-flying fighter jets over the Labrador forest, this type of life, bound to nature, is no more. The villages on the coast of Labrador have become a sort of sociological laboratory in which bureaucrats conduct experiments with new forms of economic redemption dressed in euphemistic names that give them a vague, reassuring flavour, a taste of the future.

In Canada, as elsewhere, there is much debate over the fate of Amazonian tribes whose land is being deforested, and whose way of life is disappearing. But what will become of *us*, in our hyper-technological society, cut off from nature, when an unforeseen breakdown in machinery brings us up short against this rude reality: we have lost the basic techniques for survival (making fire with two pieces of wood, for example, or, in a science-fiction future, reproducing by copulation)? The Amazonian natives certainly have first-hand knowledge of what scientific progress is destroying. Yet so do the Labradorians, even cross-bred with the descendants of the Vikings, and the Newfoundlanders in the outports, and all the people who live close to the elements—farmers, fishermen, hunters—whom the laws of the market are relegating to folklore by decimating their environment without anyone so much as murmuring a protest.

We always feel better when we find the fleas on our neighbours.

3

Newfoundland: a product of the fishery

THE SAD SAGA OF NEWFOUNDLAND is that the collapse of the cod stocks is killing it. Not just ruining its economy, but assassinating its identity and its soul.

In what state of disrepair will Newfoundlanders find themselves at the end of the eighteen-month moratorium decreed by the Canadian government on the very eve of the hundred-and-twenty-fifth anniversary of Confederation? Twenty thousand people, out of a population of just half a million, will lose their jobs for at least a year and a half, as the fishery will not be re-opened until a new scientific evaluation indicates that northern cod populations have recovered sufficiently to be exploited again.

Should we be surprised that Canada's jubilee was celebrated nowhere in St. John's, Gander, or Port-aux-Basques on the first of July, that people's faces were morose, sullen, sour, and that they were fed up with the big, beautiful country *a mari usque ad mare* to which they had attached themselves with a faint heart (51 per cent of votes after two referendums) just forty-three years ago? In the opinion of many Newfoundlanders, the cod-fishery moratorium was the result of disastrous management of the fish populations by the central power in Ottawa, which they perceived as an army of incompetent, arrogant bureaucrats that unceasingly sprouted tentacle-like departments, divisions, services, and subservices even as the cod, and the fishermen, disappeared. And all the while, the civil servants remained obstinately deaf and blind to the fishermen's warnings—mostly small inshore fishermen, the true experts in the ecology of the Grand Banks, who had drawn their subsistence from the sea for generations.

The imposed cessation of the primary economic activity in Newfoundland was a very bitter pill to swallow. Nor did the sugar coating of a half-billion dollars in palliative economic aid make things any easier: getting between two and four hundred dollars a week to sit back and wait was cold comfort indeed. Pride cannot be bought. And isn't the best way to kill a man, or a people, as Félix Leclerc wrote, to pay them to do nothing?

To understand the true depth of the tragedy, one must understand that as much as it is a producer of fish, Newfoundland is a product of the fishery.

Even before the great explorers—Cabot, Cortereal, Cartier—came to confirm the discoveries made by early sailor-fishermen and to take possession of new territories in the names of their respective sovereigns, the Bretons, the Welsh, the Gaels, the Galicians, the Basques, and others knew about the phenomenal abundance of fish on the Banks of Newfoundland. By the time Giovanni Caboto (John Cabot, as the British called him) returned from a trip, that had probably taken him to Cape Breton, and reported to the king of England that his ship could not move through the water so thick was it with cod, they were already there, fishing. (Not to tarnish the accomplishments of these famous navigators, we must remember that they were not looking primarily for rich new fishing grounds, the existence of which were already known, but for a passage to the famous kingdom of Cathay and its fabulous wealth, a search in which North America, placed awkwardly in their path, was but a giant geographic obstacle.)

In fact, Jacques Cartier met Breton fishermen at the entrance to the Strait of Belle-Isle on his very first voyage. The Basques built whale-oil melting-stations in Labrador and on the north coast of the Gulf of St. Lawrence before the Great Voyages. The Vikings' sagas tell of their landing on Vinland (Newfoundland) at the turn of the millennium. And an Irish monk named Brendan left an account of a fabulous voyage that also took him to Newfoundland in the eighth century on board a ship made of leather.

It seems that the English came to fish on the Grand Banks as early as 1481, and we know for certain that the Portuguese fished there in 1501. There are indications that the Vikings visited the waters of George's Bank and Nantucket Bank, in the Gulf of Maine, even earlier.

Once the great discoveries were made, what had been a well-guarded secret of fishermen and scholars was struck with the royal seal and became public knowledge. The true revolution came with the invention of the printing press, which permitted the rapid distribution of information. While Friar Brendan's text and the Scandinavian sagas were manuscripts laboriously copied by hand, few in number and jealously preserved by the monks, Jacques Cartier's accounts of his voyage and John Cabot's log were soon printed and read by the hundreds and thousands.

With no further prodding, owners of European fishing fleets took great risks to multiply their fishing trips to the Grand Banks. All the more ships were sent to fish there because the Roman Catholic calendar of the time had a bewildering number of lean days, and the schools of cod, the fish favoured on these days, were quickly being exhausted in the eastern Atlantic.

This is how Newfoundland was populated. Every spring, around March or April, the codfishing ships sailed from European ports for the rich fishing grounds of the new continent. There were already more than 125 of them before 1550. At the end of the sixteenth century, with their numbers growing, cod landings on the Grand Banks were up to a hundred thousand tonnes per year. A century later, landings had doubled, and during the nineteenth century, still with rudimentary technology, the take varied, depending on the year, between 150,000 and 400,000 tonnes per fishing season.

The European fishing schooners stopped first in the Gulf of Maine or the Gulf of St. Lawrence to take herring to bait their lines, then went to the Grand Banks and fished for cod until bad autumn weather or full holds forced them to return to their home port.

Their fishing technique, still practised by some countries at the beginning of the 1960s, was similar to inshore fishing, except that instead of leaving shore every morning, the fishing boats left a mother ship. They were lowered into the water by the catheads and headed out in all directions on the immense ocean, usually with two men on board, to work at sea all day. The first task, early in the morning, was to pull up their long lines, unhook the cod, rebait the hooks with pieces of herring or mackerel, and set them down again between their buoys; then, once the catch was gutted and washed, the livers saved, they went on jigging.

Toward the end of the afternoon, earlier if their boat was full, they went back to the mother ship, where they washed their catch again and salted it in large brine barrels. Then they ate and sacked out on their bunks, in the forecastle, getting as much sleep as they could, for the moment the stars faded the next morning, the pitiless bosun's whistle would rouse them from their dreams of gentle moors with gorse and flowers and of maidens of Paimpol, with hair fairer than their sails, awaiting them back home in Brittany.

If we just substitute Newfoundland for Iceland and Newfoundlander for Icelander in Théodore Botrel's famous song, we would have a feel for life on these ships.

[. . .]
The brave Icelander, without a sound,
Throws out his line and his harpoon,
Later, in the briny stench,
Below-decks on his narrow bench . . .
The poor soul sighs
As down he lies:
"I'd be much happier, it's so true,
In front of a fire orange and blue,
Holding hands with my Paimpol lady,
Who awaits me in Britanny!"

But often the sea that he rides
Awakes him, cruel and wide,
And when evening falls they toll
All the names that don't answer the roll . . .
And the poor tar chants
Under his breath:
"To fight the English fleet, my friend
We'll need more hands, more strong young men,
I'll talk it over with my Paimpol lady
When I get back to Britanny!"*
. . .]

Work on a Newfoundland fishing boat was fraught with
danger. The boats, open dories, sometimes ranged very far
from the mother ship. The fishermen competed for the
largest catch; since they wanted to hide the secret of their
grounds, they often hid from each other, beyond the horizon,
but also beyond the view of the lookout man perched in the
crow's-nest on the mizzen-mast. In good weather, when the
powerful swell gently rocked like a cradle in a sort of protean

---

*Here is the original French text :
Le brave Islandais, sans murmure
Jette la ligne et le harpon:
Puis dans un relent de saumure,
Il se couche dans l'entrepont . . .
Et le pauvre gars
Soupire tout bas:
«Je serions bien mieux à mon aise
«Devant un joli feu d'ajonc,
« À côté de la Paimpolaise
«Qui m'attend au pays breton!»

Mais souvent l'océan qu'il dompte
Se réveille, lâche et cruel;
Et, lorsque le soir on se compte
Bien des noms manquent à l'appel . . .
Et le pauvre gars
Fredonne tout bas:
«Pour combattre la flotte anglaise
«Comme il faut plus d'un moussaillon,
«J'en caus'rons à ma Paimpolaise,
«En rentrant au pays breton!»

oceanic respiration, this was not a problem. But when the thick fogs for which the Grand Banks are famous rolled in, and the wind raised huge waves that tossed the ships and chased the little dories with fangs of foam, beware to those who had ventured too far! Especially when the wind's ferocious howling and the roar of breakers exploding in spumes of spray kept them from hearing the horn of the mother ship desperately calling out to its lost children.

As night fell on such days, there were always fishermen who did not answer the roll-call. Estimating where they had drifted from the strength and direction of the wind, the mother ship would go in search of them as soon as the ocean calmed down in the area where they were thought to be or should have been, but they were not always found. The ocean is vast; on the high seas, it is amazing how all horizons and swells look alike.

The danger involved in the high-seas fishery is perhaps one reason that British, French, Portuguese, and Spanish sailors touched down on *terra firma*. Newfoundland, the Rock, its coast furrowed with bights and deep coves, offered a base of operations infinitely more stable and comfortable than the bridge of a ship. There was no lack of cod anywhere, and the catches to be had a few miles from the capes and the farthest reefs were comparable to those on the high seas. Besides, why risk the perilous voyage to Europe every autumn when they would only be returning the following spring? Moreover, the cabins and other installations had already been built and needed to be guarded against pirates and savages.

The English had their own particular motives for visiting the coast. With scarce salt reserves back home, and perhaps also because of their very rainy autumns, they salted their catch only lightly and preserved the fish by drying it in the sun on the stony beaches of the *New Founde Lande*. The fishermen of other countries, having an abundance of salt and the Mediterranean sun in the autumn, preserved their catch in salty brine, so that it did not require immediate drying. This process produced what is called green cod.

As well, there was the prospect, for poor ocean labourers, that they could suddenly become landowners, just like bluebloods—even if the land in question was but a piece of this miserable, barren coast. For a taste of the freedom denied them in their country of origin, more and more fishermen settled on land in spite of the laws and injunctions on board most of the fishing ships which forbade it. Newfoundland, "the great ship moored near the fishing banks", thus progressively became a sort of multi-national crypto-colony. Fishermen and their families set down roots in the bights and recesses of the capricious coast. Thanks to a remarkably high birth rate, settlement on the Rock proceeded apace.

The place names of the island suggest, in a general way, the national origins of the first European inhabitants of the coast: British, French, Iberian. But, beyond the rivalries and alliances of their home countries, the colonists soon forged an identity as true Newfoundlanders, a people who lived for and by the sea.

And, it must be said, exclusively the sea. This fact made it a *different* society, distinct from all others that settled in North America. In contrast to colonists in other regions, the first Newfoundlanders never penetrated the interior of their territory. They didn't clear land to make fields for agriculture. They didn't even bother to give names to the most obvious geophysical characteristics of the back country. Only the coastal features, the bights and capes and points and bays, were named. In fact, the land was thought of only as a platform from which to exploit the marine wealth, which Newfoundlanders considered their property even though it was submerged by the sea.

As Dr. Leslie Harris notes in the *Independent Review of the State of the Northern Cod Stock (1990)*, ethnological research has shown that the first colonists chose the sites where they would settle only as a function of a combination of geographic, oceanographic, and biological factors, the minimal necessary conditions being a conjuncture of winds, tides, and currents that favoured easy access to the fish-laden waters by sail or by oar, sufficient beach on which to dry the catch, and an adequate supply of fresh water. The first sites occupied were neither the best-sheltered harbours nor those in proximity to arable land. The essential criterion was accessibility to the fishing banks.

Thus was shaped and constructed the Newfoundland soul: a mosaic of people spread over more than a thousand small communities sprinkled around a coastline of more than ten thousand kilometres, ferociously attached to their bit of beach or their cape plunging into the ocean, and wedded to the marine resources.

As if by imitation, the people who attached themselves to the Rock acquired its resilience and solidity. Over three or four centuries (we must not forget that St. John's is the oldest city in North America), Newfoundlanders acquired not only strength, endurance, independence, and courage, but also the altruism, sense of community, equanimity, and humour they needed to survive in such harsh conditions. These qualities were woven into a pattern of national identity, an insular mystique, which can only crumble in the absence of the activity that sustains it: codfishing.

The human tragedy resulting from the accelerated industrialization of the fishery over the last thirty-odd years has culminated in the progressive extinction both of the inshore fishermen, the historical guardians of the fishing resource, and of the cod stocks.

Without the fishery, during the eighteen-month moratorium imposed by Ottawa, the very soul of Newfoundland cannot help but continue to wither away. The vigorous small communities that formed the warp and weft of the Rock's social fabric, already badly wounded, some slowly dying because of the decline in resources, have finally ground to a standstill.

This is much more than just economic and social difficulties; it is a true cultural genocide that threatens the population of the island today.

4

Gadus morhua and Homo Erectus

THE SPECIES *GADUS MORHUA*, called *cabillaud* by European francophones before it is salted, *bacalao* in Spain, and *bacalhau* in Portugal, is found in the depths of all northern oceans. It is present in the European continental shelf, around Iceland and Greenland, on the northwest banks of the Atlantic, and in the Pacific. The latter (*morhua macrocephalus*) is called charcoal cod because of its darker, almost black skin. The Atlantic cod has a mottled, light greenish-grey skin, sometimes tinted brown or red, depending on its habitat. It has three dorsal and two anal fins, and a barbel under its chin. A slightly wavy line runs along its body from the gills to the tail. On average, an adult cod weighs two to three kilos and measures about seventy centimetres in length; since it never stops growing, it can be much larger and heavier, though usually not more than thirty kilos. The largest individual ever caught measured in excess of 1.8 metres and weighed ninety-six kilos!

Submitted to intensive fishing, cod rarely live longer than fifteen years, although a twenty-seven-year-old fish has been caught on the Labrador coast. The age of the fish is counted by the number of rings on its otolith, a small bone situated near its ear that helps with balance.

The large family of Gadidae to which the cod belongs includes the haddock, the whiting, the hake, the ling, the pollock, and freshwater and saltwater fish like the turbot, the loach, the tommy-cod, and so on.

From upper Labrador to Cape Hatteras, the North American continental shelf comprises a dozen distinct cod populations. Each population has its own seasonal migration pattern; generally, the cod are found in the deep water (between 200 and 600 metres) of the continental slope in the winter, and in shallow coastal waters in the summer. If the deeps are not far away, like at Flemish Cap, east of the Grand Banks, where an independent population of cod lives, the migration is a short one; the fish descend to the deeper waters of the Flemish Cap slope in the winter and move to its summit in the summer. Other stocks, like the one that lives in the south of the Gulf of St. Lawrence in the summer, travel hundreds of nautical miles—in this case, to the water holes of Scatarie Island—in the winter.

Fishermen have had a very good idea of these migratory movements for a long time. The intensive tagging programmes undertaken by marine biologists, especially since the mid-1960s, only gave the scientific seal of approval to what fishermen already knew, and perhaps contributed this essential knowledge to fishery management: the same cod travel the same migratory paths year after year, and therefore are part of distinct populations or stocks. It is even possible that some of these populations, sharing the same waters in the summer, are sufficiently different genetically that they cannot interbreed.

The cod populations spawn at various locations between March and May, continuing until June in some zones of the Grand Banks. The females, which reach sexual maturity at around six years of age, release between two and eleven million eggs each measuring one to two millimetres in diameter; once fertilized, the eggs float up to the surface, where they are at the mercy of the wind, the currents, and numerous predators. It is estimated that out of the millions of eggs produced by a female, only one ends up becoming an adult fish to ensure survival of the species.

To study cod reproduction, Norwegian ethologists enclosed with netting from the surface to the sea bed a large spawning ground and installed underwater night-vision television cameras. Egg laying seems to be linked to certain criteria of salinity and water temperature (between 2.5° and 4° Celsius at the bottom), and these conditions are found at depths a little shallower on their side of the Atlantic than on the slope of the North American continental shelf, because of the influence of the Gulf

Stream. This greatly facilitates observation.

The ethologists observed that the male prepares the equivalent of a nest for the female. He cleans impurities, swallowing any sediments, plankton, small shellfish, and algae that he finds, from a column of water of which he seems to recognize the perimeter. From the bottom to the surface, he turns in this space, rising in a spiral; when the invisible nest is rid of all foreign bodies, he goes back down to the bottom and awaits the female. If at this point one lets drop the smallest object—a bit of shell, a pebble—in his cleaned column of water, he quickly swims away, as if frightened, and begins again elsewhere. This shows how much fishing, even of other species, in the spawning grounds at spawning time can harm the cod.

The female seems to recognize the water nest prepared by the male, since she tarries, also circling, and performing certain swimming patterns that must be signals designed to attract the male's attention as he lies in wait at the bottom of his column. The male then rises toward the female and, swimming on his back beneath her, shadows her movements. They get closer and closer until their bellies touch. Then he brings out from his anal region a minuscule penis which enters the orifice of the female. Soon she releases a cloud of eggs, which the male sprinkles with his semen.

After they hatch, the larvae, about half a centimetre long, feed on the egg yolk, which remains attached to their abdomen, for two weeks; after this, they must find their own food. When the fry reach four centimetres in length, at the age of one to two months, depending on the population, they sojourn in the depths of relatively shallow waters, near the coast. They favour the deep bays of the Newfoundland coast. At one year of age, they are ten to twenty centimetres long.

But all cod do not grow at the same pace. Northern cod grow much more slowly than their southern cousins; even within one population, growth may vary according to different factors: water temperature, abundance of food, and the density of the school. Accordingly, cod that winter in the Scatarie Island water holes grow less quickly during the sum-

mer in the Gulf of St. Lawrence than in the Gulf of Maine,
south of Nova Scotia.

When they are four years old, the cod of southern Nova
Scotia are already, on average, fifty centimetres long and
weigh a kilo. Since they are too large to escape through the
mesh of the trawl, they can now be fished. The Labrador cod
reach this size only two years later, and will never get larger
than an average of sixty-five centimetres in length and 1.5
kilos in weight. Thus, at eight years of age, Labrador cod
weigh only a third of those from south of the Grand Banks; at
twelve years of age, only a quarter. This means that a greater
number of individuals are killed per tonne caught, and thus,
the biomass is slower to rebuild when they are overfished.

All of these biological facts are, of course, very useful for
understanding the dynamics of cod-stock populations and
deciding fishing seasons, but they don't reveal much about a
crucial element that determines tolerable levels of resource
exploitation: *biomass*. The problem is that with the data
available (catch reported per fishing zone, by fishing vessels,
etc., and samples taken of the catches by research vessels in
order to establish the composition of stocks by age), we cannot determine the biomass with any degree of precision except in hindsight, after the fish have been caught.

The method, called virtual population analysis (VPA), is relatively simple. It consists of listing, year after year, the number of
fish caught from each age class and adjusting this number upward slightly to account for estimated natural mortality. Let's
take, for example, individuals born in 1975, what is called the
1975 recruitment: in 1978, analysis of the catches by age class
shows that a certain number of these fish, now three years old,
have been landed. In 1979, the quantity of four-year-olds caught
is counted; in 1980, the five-year-olds; in 1981, the six-year-
olds; and so on, up to 1988 or until the sampling of catches reveals no significant percentage of cod from the 1975
recruitment. Thus, the total of fish recruited to the stock in
1975 is determined by simply accumulating data on them
through the years. If the count has been accurate and if the na-
tural-mortality rate has been correctly calculated each year, one

can have a good approximate idea of the number of cod born in 1975. A similar process is followed for all age classes.

This method of evaluating stocks cannot give any idea at all of the quantity of fish living in the ocean at the present. It provides us with more or less accurate figures on the quantity caught from each age class; how many remain in the sea is, at best, a guess. In an attempt to quantify this guess (*guess*timating, in oceanologists' jargon), the biologists calculate a value, F (instantaneous mortality through fishing), based on historical mortality rates attributable to fishing by age class, thus on an analysis of the composition of catches over a certain period of time, which can easily be equated to a proportion of total exploitable populations. Only later, however, when all the individuals of a particular age class have been fished, can one know if the value ascribed to F was correct; if it was not, it must be readjusted for future evaluations. Of course, it is understood that the more abundant, varied, and longitudinal the historical data, the more likely the value F is to be correct.

To evaluate permissible catch rates for a fish population each year, the scientists "tune", or adjust, the basic data provided by the VPA with as many parameters as possible, notably surveys of fish schools performed by research vessels and catch per unit of effort (CPUE) reports supplied by trawlers' logs. The research vessels take samples from trawls of equal duration conducted at different depths, or strata, of the fish schools. The catch at each location and stratum is analyzed to establish its age and weight structure. These data are then used to estimate the age structure of the fish school, the number of individuals it contains, and its biomass, and these figures are extrapolated to describe the entire population of a particular stock. Similarly, CPUE reports measure the trawlers' catch as a function of time spent trawling and are used to derive indexes regarding the entire population, under the assumption that there is in fact a relationship between the CPUE and the size of this population.

Obviously, these are epistemologically weak tools, but they are the only ones available for studying biological phenomena of unimaginable complexity that take place out of sight, under vast expanses of water. The fishery manager's job sometimes resembles that of the sorcerer's apprentice. He must use his science although it is still in the development stage and, like all science, gropes its way forward through an experimental sequence of trial and error. Except that, in this case, errors are very costly. Too few studies, a wrinkle in odds probability that means that a sample taken at random is not representative of the whole, an overly narrow analysis of the statistical data, the lack of a historical perspective, the exclusion of certain factors (environmental, ecological, and others) whose pertinence may be underestimated, and the entire rationale of the fishery quota system could collapse or mutate in a crazy aberration, with unsuspected, catastrophic, and irreparable consequences for the future.

The science, or art, of the biometricist consists of determining the maximum possible exploitation of the stocks while ensuring their sustained yield over the long term (MSY, or maximum sustainable yield). In short, this consists of taking the fish after it has reproduced as many times as possible and before it dies a natural death.

If we can estimate the population dynamics of different fish stocks under specific fishing conditions, and if we know the migratory paths of these stocks, all we need do to manage the fishery is divide the ocean into zones corresponding to the habitat of these stocks. Thus, the northern Atlantic has been cut into geometric sections identified by a number and one or two letters (see map), which trace roughly the geographic division of the various cod populations and their seasonal movements.

Now we must allocate catch quotas to each management zone for each season in order to ensure that the fish are not exploited beyond their sustainability. Although these zones were determined by research on the cod stocks, they are also used to manage the fishing of other species, such as redfish, scallops, shrimp, flatfish, and so on, because they delineate, again roughly, the distribution of various fishing grounds. Management by geographic unit also permits maintenance of the essential ecological balance between species in order to ensure the long-term biological yield of the area, on which the rationale of the fishery is based.

It must be noted that the notion of ecological balance between species is itself deceptive, because every ecosystem is a dynamic entity that tends toward balance without ever achieving it.

Humans were added to the list of predators of the western Atlantic cod only toward the middle of the last millennium. Neither the aboriginals of Newfoundland, the Beothuks, nor the Micmacs who populated Nova Scotia, the Gaspé peninsula, and New Brunswick seem to have cared much for this fish. They undoubtedly occasionally snared cod in their nets, but their taste ran more to salmon.

Cod was principally the prey of fish larger than itself, such as halibut; some marine mammals such as seals, walruses, porpoises, and a few other fish-eating cetaceans; sharks; and the occasional bear. A large number of individuals, especially in the larval stage, fall prey to cannibalism. Although all of these predatory species, including cod itself, were more abundant before the coming of the white man than they are now, the cod probably had an easier time and lived, on the whole, to an older age than today, populating the schools with a much higher proportion of very large individuals.

The arrival of Europeans brought the dawn of a new era. While the aboriginals who had lived in Newfoundland for seven or eight millennia could not, with their sparse population and primitive technology, significantly alter the balance of marine life, the Europeans, through their numbers and the nature of their civilization, expanding territorially and metamorphosing technologically, had the potential to do so. As I mentioned in the previous chapter, fishing the North American cod populations quickly led to colonization of Newfoundland and other parts of the east coast of North America.

The cod was aptly nicknamed "Newfoundland cash", as was proclaimed on an early one-cent stamp that bears its likeness, and its economic importance was acknowledged elsewhere as well: Cape Cod bears its name, a wood sculpture of a codfish adorns the Massachusetts House of Representatives in Boston, and a piece of change struck to commemorate the visit of Seigneur Coffin to his fief on the Magdalen Islands early in the last century (1806), had the image of a dried cod on the reverse and that of a seal on the obverse.

After remaining stable at between 100,000 and 150,000 tonnes per year during the seventeenth and eighteenth centuries, cod catches increased during the nineteenth century, and 400,000 tonnes may have been landed in the best years. These figures are, of course, only estimates, because the fishing countries did not start to keep statistics until relatively late: 1869 for Canada, 1874 for France, 1896 for Portugal, and so on. The only means of evaluating the extent of the fishery before this time is to analyze the records of exporters, importers, and fish merchants, taking account that weights given are only for finished products—salted (green) or dried cod—which must be converted into live weight.

But whether this conversion factor is estimated at 3 or 3.93 (depending on the author), the catch had no dramatic effect on the vitality of the stocks. The relatively primitive technology used guaranteed that what was fished remained well below the sustainable level. After all, the only fish that bit at the hooks were those greedy enough to do so and large enough to swallow the bait, and the only fish harpooned by the jigger were those that had the misfortune to find themselves within the perimeter of its lethal triangle, which is a mere four centimetres per side.

It was, in fact, only at the beginning of the twentieth century that the true enemy of the fish, and in the long run of the fishermen, appeared: I'm talking about the trawler.

5

The Trawlers

THE IDEA OF HARVESTING FISH by towing a net along the ocean bottom was certainly not a new one. Shrimp fishermen on both sides of the English Channel, Flemish and British, had long used a primitive trawl consisting of a pocket of netting attached to a hardwood beam weighted with iron that was pulled by a horse in shallow waters at low tide. Today a vanished tradition—magnificent on their huge horses, with their oilskins and sou'westers, filling the baskets attached to the animal's harness with shrimp—these fishermen were still making a living off the sea in the 1950s.

By 1896, the beam trawl had been adapted to towing in deeper waters by steamboats, but because it was rigid it could not be used in grounds that were not sandy and flat. The next innovation was to anchor the net with a large chain, equipped with wheel-like bobbins at regular intervals, on which it rolled along the ocean floor. This apparatus, the otter trawl, opened vertically thanks to floats and laterally thanks to doors attached to the towing cables, which wiggled in the water.

A European invention, it was many years before the trawler, or dragger, crossed the Atlantic. The great coal reserves required by the voyage took space in the hold that could not be devoted to fish. As well, traditions die hard on the ocean. Many countries continued to fish by sail up to the inter-war period, and the last codfishing schooners finally disappeared from the horizons of the Grand Banks only as late as the 1950s.

By this time, the sailing ships were utterly anachronistic, for there was a sharp rise in the fishing effort of the various fleets. By the end of the Second World War, there were no longer several dozen, but hundreds of European ships crossing the Atlantic each year to take fish from the Grand Banks and the Gulf of St. Lawrence. According to international maritime law, they could fish as close to the coast as twelve nautical miles.

And the draggers were everywhere, thumbing their noses at the Canadian fishing ships, the largest of which were still modest longliners and gillnetters, such as the famous *Gaspésienne*, designed by Howard Chapel.

So as not to lag behind the foreigners (the expansion of the offshore fishery inevitably caused a corresponding atrophy in the inshore fishery), fishermen in Atlantic Canada and on the American coast also intensified their fishing efforts, using more and larger draggers. Annual cod catches of 800,000, 900,000, and even approaching 1,000,000 tonnes became the rule during the 1950s.

If the average weight of each cod caught was 2.5 kilos, this meant that each year 320 to 400 million individuals were removed from the fishery. Could the stocks sustain such a mortality rate? Alarmed scientists in the fishing countries began to study the possible effects of such a considerable exploitation of the fish reserves of the northwest Atlantic. This led to the formation, in 1952, of the International Commission for the Northwest Atlantic Fisheries (ICNAF), a United Nations agency comprising Canada, the United States, Spain, Portugal, the U.S.S.R., Poland, Norway, France, Italy, Bulgaria, East and West Germany, Cuba, Japan, and other countries.

ICNAF was created to discipline countries that abused the resource, but it quickly fell victim to the difficulties inherent in implementing policies that apply to a number of nations. Without any true coercive power, and because the activity it was intended to regulate took place in the juridical no-man's-land of international waters, ICNAF could at first only obtain the consent of its members only to regulate the mesh size of the trawls (albeit inadequately!) to permit undersized fish to escape. On the other hand, it had to depend on the good will of each member country to ensure that the standards were respected.

In any case, the regulations did not cool the fishing ardour of the fleets. By 1960, cod catches on the banks of Newfoundland, Nova Scotia, and the Gulf of St. Lawrence totalled over a million tonnes per year, and they kept growing throughout the decade to reach almost two million tonnes in 1968 —1,900,000 tonnes, in fact. Meanwhile, it was already being noticed that the size of cod caught was diminishing. The fish "as big as a man", that all the inshore fisherman recalled with a tremor in their voices and the respect paid to a cherished past, were found less and less frequently. This meant that for the same tonnage, many more individuals were being destroyed, among them potential breeding stock. The ineluctable cycle of decline had begun. At the end of the 1960s, the equivalent of today's total biomass, and more, was being caught each year!

The catching power of the foreign fishing fleets in these years is illustrated by the story of the Magdalen Islands captain of a small, twenty-metre trawler, the *Colombe*. In the autumn, he was trawling near Cape Breton Island, in a well-stocked fishing ground that was overrun with Canadian and foreign draggers. At one point, although he was trawling full steam ahead, he had the impression that he wasn't moving forward, but backward. When the first moment of incredulity passed, he realized that a huge trawler flying the Italian flag, as he recalls it, had crossed a little too close astern, caught his cables and doors, and was pulling him—his trawl on the sea floor, the fish in his hold, and his boat, with the engine running full steam in the opposite direction—as if he were a simple rowboat!

When he made a radio call in what he felt was a suitably indignant tone, the captain of the Italian dragger replied calmly, wondering why he was so upset. It couldn't have been so terrible, after all: the Italian had felt absolutely nothing; his ship was going its usual speed on a regular trawling run. He even found it rather amusing that the *Colombe* was along for the ride.

It was senseless, wild overfishing, and in 1969 annual cod catches dropped for the first time, to 1,500,000 tonnes. This trend was confirmed the following year (1,150,000 tonnes), and the catch continued to tumble throughout the decade, finally reaching the same levels—below 500,000 tonnes in 1976, 1977, and 1978—as those achieved at the end of the nineteenth century by a fishing fleet a fraction of the size and with nothing like the same technological arsenal. An analysis of the catch in the 1960s also reveals a growing share of northern cod in the total landings, no doubt because the other stocks were no longer offering a satisfactory yield.

The fishing grounds situated within the Gulf of St. Lawrence and the Bay of Fundy had in fact been so depleted of cod that other countries raised only feeble protests when Canada, in 1972, proclaimed these two zones "interior seas" and placed them under its exclusive jurisdiction. It was simply no longer profitable for the large foreign units to trawl for so few fish! The European fleets concentrated their efforts on the Grand Banks of Newfoundland, and took large catches of northern cod in 1972 and 1974 (400,000 tonnes and more— half of the total cod landings in the northwest Atlantic in these years consisted of northern cod). With this overfishing, the northern cod stock, the very stock that fifteen years later would justify the closing of the Newfoundland fishery, collapsed a first time.

This is an important fact, usually ignored in discussions of overfishing today.

These first disasters provoked ICNAF to impose national quotas on cod takes in 1973. But, just as with verification of mesh size, ICNAF had no effective means of ensuring the quotas, nor recourse against countries that ignored them and whose landing reports indicated that they were vastly exceeding the allocations.

By 1973, overfishing had plunged all of the Atlantic provinces into a serious crisis, which they weathered only with massive aid from the federal government to support the fishery industries until the stocks improved. If we take into account the devaluation of the Canadian dollar, the aid package for the eighteen-month moratorium on cod fishing cost the public purse a half-billion dollars spread over three years.

Nevertheless, at the time, there was still optimism. People talked as if there were a panacea for all of Canada's cod problems: extension of Canada's exclusive jurisdiction to an economic zone extending two hundred nautical miles from shore—"and farther", according to the preliminary texts.

First proposed by a number of coastal nations, including Canada, at the Caracas session of the Convention on the Law of the Sea, this request was reiterated at the Geneva session, and was finally adopted on 1 January 1977. But it was adopted without the crucial final words of the original proposal, *and farther*, which meant that the Flemish Cap, the Nose and the Tail of the Grand Banks, and the continental slope, where the cod migrated in winter, escaped Canada's exclusive jurisdiction.

The decline in fish populations had a perverse consequence: improvements in harvesting techniques. To make fishing trips profitable, larger and more effective trawlers were developed, and their fishing gear was technologically upgraded, notably with regard to fish locating and catching power. This devastated even further the remaining stocks. In order to avoid ripping the trawls on the rough sea bottom, a midwater trawl was developed, which is towed at high speed.

Thanks to the colour echo sounder, not only can the captain of a fishing vessel see the depth at which the fish are found and determine the length, width, and thickness of the school, he can even get a good idea of the species, fish size, and so on. All he then has to do is lower his trawl to the indicated stratum—a trawl with a gaping mouth the size of a football field—and fill it. His main concern, when he finds such abundance, is to decide when to raise his net; if it is too full it rips at the surface and all the fish tumble into the sea in a red or silver tide, depending on the species being fished. This is a loss for everyone except the gulls, and especially for the captain, whose crew must then spend long hours resewing and repairing the rigging, therefore losing fishing time. And time is money.

To avoid this serious problem, the trawl mouth is equipped with a sensor that measures the quantity of fish entering. But this does not eliminate the sin of gluttony—the famous syndrome common to all fishermen, from the Sunday angler to the trawler captain—and there are always those who, wanting to catch more and do better, catch too much and make things worse.

So far, I have been talking about Canadian ship sizes: trawlers usually forty to fifty metres in length, which constitute the main body of large high-seas fishing vessels, towing trawls with an open mouth the size of a football field. But these are by no means the most powerful fishing vessels. They look like small skiffs beside the giant draggers, the floating fish factories of the ex-U.S.S.R., Germany, France, and Spain. These mammoth ships 100 to 150 metres long, with engines boasting horsepower in the thousands, raise fish by the tens of tonnes at a time, using colossal winches, chains, and cables.

The Spanish draggers work in pairs, pulling between them a trawl measuring about a mile and a half in length, which sweeps up all the fish in its way and destroys great quantities of organisms—plants, shellfish, mollusks, cnidaria, and so on—that colonize the ocean depths and play an important role in the food chain. In turn, first one ship then the other lifts and empties the trawl, so that each crew has double the time to sort, gut, wash, and salt the cod. Underwater photographs of the depths swept by these gigantic nets reveal denuded, desert-like spaces on which are imprinted, like a symbol of their decimation, the tracks of the huge rubber bobbins on which the trawls roll.

The race to technological innovation seems to know no end. Today, the bridge of even the smallest trawler is awash with high-technology instruments. From port to starboard, there are computer screens, colour sonar screens, radar screens —tens of thousands of dollars worth of them. On more sophisticated units, the antique, well-worn helm wheel has disappeared, along with the compass whose magnetized point always indicated north: these vessels sail on electronic pilot and navigate by a satellite signal that gives coordinates to the metre almost anywhere on the surface of the globe.

As for the science of the fisherman, which was based on a experienced knowledge of the sea, transmitted from generation to generation, it has been replaced by technology: powerful scanners, lasers, and sensors of all sorts that reveal the most intimate secrets of the abyss, including underwater cameras that send live pictures to the bridge screens showing sea life, if any, under the ship's hull.

The Spanish, who are prolific fishermen, have just developed trawls that fish to a depth of 1,400 metres—four times deeper than most Canadian ships. They are also developing computerized, intelligent trawls, which don't get hooked and tear on the craggy ocean floor, but coiling up and down like a snake, hug the rough spots, the ditches and rises, the thorns of the deep.

Thus, the fish are no longer protected by the natural element of the topography of the depths, and they are being caught even where Canadian biologists thought they were beyond reach!

There are disturbing corollaries to this race to high technology. The first is that one does not necessarily have to be a fisherman to work on high-tech trawlers. Anyone who is used to manipulating heavy industrial machinery and has sea legs can fish. Once, to be a fisherman meant having a certain sensitivity for the sea and its resources, on which one's livelihood depended. For the trawler worker, these considerations mean little: the paycheque comes first.

The second corollary is that this equipment is very expensive and requires a considerable investment, much higher than can be committed even by the most prosperous fishing enterprises, so they must borrow massively to equip a modern fleet. This means that in the final analysis it is financial imperatives—the bankers, really—that determine, or at least strongly influence, the intensity of the fishing effort.

The technological aspect of the fishery is so highly developed, the economic imperatives so pressing, that when a large school of fish is located, there is a strong chance that not one individual will escape being caught. It must be noted that in these cod-poor years, schools can be located from the air. A plane equipped with the appropriate instruments is rented, a minimal investment given the colossal ships that must be made profitable. Once a school is found, the news crackles on every radio in the fleet, and soon all the ships converge on the spot, where huge catches are taken. It's carnage, pure and simple.

6

The Pillage of the Gulf

BEFORE I CONTINUE with the sad story of *Gadus morhua* at the hands of humans in the industrial era, I would like to point out that the current worldwide fishery crisis is not really new but, rather, a repetition of previous crises from which we did not learn our lessons. A good illustration of this is an article that I published in *Le Maclean* (the Québec equivalent of Maclean's) in March, 1975, after working for two winters on the trawlers as a fisherman and deck hand. Except for certain statistics, which have changed for the worse, and some major events that have occurred since, such as the institution of a two-hundred-mile economic zone, the article could have been written this year. The magazine's editors entitled it, *The Pillage of the Gulf*. The article won second prize in the 1976 Canadian Business Writing Awards given out each year by the Royal Bank of Canada and the Toronto Press Club. Here it is, translated for the first time:

Superstition warns against whistling at sea (it is said to raise bad weather), so men sing to kill time at the wheel on a long night-time trawl, when there is nothing to do but keep nose to compass and glance, when they think of it, at the sonar screen for the water depth. And it's not surprising that they don't always sing a happy ditty like *I'se the b'y that catches the fish* to get through the star-filled, horizonless night, but rather the plaintive sea shanty that goes, *I see you shining, star that guides the sailors* . . .

At dawn, as the trawl is lifted, as the cables and pulleys groan, the fisherman notes the meagre catch in the pocket of the dray and recalls when, not so long ago, he filled his hold with sixty thousand pounds of fish in two or three days. Today, he would be happy to land thirty thousand pounds after eight or ten days at sea on board his small, sixty-foot trawler.

Whether he is trawling, hauling in his lines, tending his traps, or drawing up his gillnets, the Gulf of St. Lawrence fisherman cannot help but note that every year the fish are fewer and smaller, and more expensive to catch. Of course, the value of the various species has been going up for several years, but this increase barely compensates for the reduced catch, and it compensates not at all for the phenomenal rise in expenses (maintenance, tackle, cables, ice, fuel). In fact, it seems pitifully small when compared to the increase in the retail price of fish (for cod, 300 per cent over four years).

With more and more time to reflect between each winching-up of the trawl, the fisherman is coming to realize that he, like the fish, is the victim of an economic system that no longer sees this age-old —and perilous—activity as a way to earn a living, but as a way, somehow or other, to pay dividends to shareholders.

When the shareholders are the fishermen themselves, as they are in the cooperatives, and when the government relies on their knowledge and judgment rather than on the cold calculations of technocrats, the fishing effort is rational and allows for both the economic wealth of the fisherman and stock conservation. But when the shareholders are New England capitalists who control almost the entire North American market for fish, and when the cooperatives themselves are dependent upon them for the distribution of their products, the situation quickly becomes both catastrophic and scandalous. Governments award enormous grants to these companies, whose financial concerns and thirst for profit are not tempered by any human or environmental consideration.

To illustrate this lack of consideration for the fish and for people, here is a story told to me by a fisherman at *Grande-Entrée*, on a memorable night during which six Gorton Pew draggers returned in tight formation from Newfoundland to Cap-aux-Meules after the crews unanimously decided to go on strike:

A few days before Christmas the previous year, the fishermen had just raised a large pocket of cod in the waters off Chéticamp. When the first blush of euphoria faded, they saw that the fish, though they weren't of an illegal size, were very small. Before shooting their trawl again they wanted to make sure that the company would purchase their catch; if not, they would rather put the fish back in the water and stop fishing. . . . The company gave them the green light, laughing at their scruples, and they worked like fiends to fill the hold to its 400,000-pound capacity so that they could be home for Christmas Eve. But when they returned to port, the company decided that the cod were too small to be filleted, and instead of buying at the current price of seven or eight cents a pound, it paid only half a cent, not even enough to defray the expenses of the ship; without the slightest remorse, it sent the entire cargo to the fish-meal plant.

Every crew has similar stories, and worse, and many fishermen say that the true sharks of the Gulf are not necessarily the dogfish that are caught from time to time in the trawl among the flounder, rays, cod, and redfish.

Not surprisingly, it was in the private sector of the fish industry, controlled by foreign interests, that the malaise prevailing in all eastern Canadian fisheries was manifested last year(1974). In the spring, herring fishermen in Yarmouth County, Nova Scotia, went on strike to demand a raise in landing prices from B.C. Packers (part of the Weston conglomerate). In August and September, they were joined by fishermen in southern Newfoundland striking against Booth Canadian Fisheries (a subsidiary of the American company of the same name). In November, it was the turn of fishermen on the Magdalen Islands, who struck against Gorton's Canada (a subsidiary of the powerful General Mills multinational). Meanwhile, Booth, seeing its plant at Petit-de-Grat, Cape Breton, underutilized, simply closed the plant, putting out of work the four hundred people who had been in its employ for twenty-three years.

The decrease in fish populations in the Gulf and the Atlantic, the cause of the deep anxiety and discontent among fishermen, is borne out by all the statistics. According to the most recent figures by the federal department of the Environment, landings of fish, shellfish, and mollusks on Canada's east coast amounted to 940,000 tonnes in 1972, a drop of 15 per cent from the 1,100,000 tonnes in 1971, and of 21 per cent from the

1,200,000 tonnes in 1970.* Far from indicating a recovery, the latest data published by the government for 1973 and the first six months of 1974 show an accelerated downward trend—figures which fishermen certainly didn't need to see to be aware of it!—especially in certain species, such as redfish, herring, cod, and scallops. Only 29,300 pounds of the latter were caught in the first six months of 1974, compared to 78,600 pounds for the same period in 1973.

On the Pacific coast, which accounts for about 15 per cent of Canadian landings but 34 per cent of the landed value, the situation of the fishery is clearly better. There, takes grew by 47 per cent from 1971 to 1972 (due to an abundance of cohoe salmon and an increase in certain herring quotas) to reach 170,000 tons, and the total value of the take rose 28 per cent, from $133 million to $145 million.

The revival of the west coast fisheries caused not a little jealousy among the east coast fishermen, who felt that it had taken place at their expense, thanks to the favouritism of the former federal minister of the Environment, Jack Davis, an M.P. from Vancouver. As the inshore fishermen from Petite Madeleine and elsewhere in the Gaspé who, in the summer of 1970, had opened fire on the giant B.C. Packers ships that had come through the Panama Canal to devastate their herring schools (to make fish meal) with six-hundred-ton nets, remarked, "Herring is doing very well on the west coast since they manage it by coming to fish ours!"

Obviously, their bullets only scratched the paint of the steel-hulled ships that they wanted to chase away, but the salvos were not completely in vain, since they awakened public opinion to the scandal of the pillage of the Gulf by all sorts of fishing ships flying foreign flags (and beside which even our large 150-foot trawlers looked like small skiffs).

The following year, the federal government passed legislation to go into effect at the beginning of 1972. Under this law, the waters of the Gulf of St. Lawrence and the Bay of

---

* Compare, as well to the 1,900,000 tonnes of cod alone taken in 1968.

Fundy would be considered Canadian interior seas and would fall under Canada's exclusive jurisdiction with regard to granting fishing and other marine rights. Fishing countries (Spain, Portugal, Italy, Japan, Norway, Russia, Poland, and West Germany, to name just a few) did not find it difficult to recognize the legitimacy of this law and renounced their historical fishing rights, which they had acquired by fishing in these waters more intensively than the country now claiming sovereignty over them! Only three countries (Great Britain, because Canada is a dominion of the British Crown, France because it possesses Saint-Pierre and Miquelon, and the United States, because it absorbs 69 per cent of Canadian fish exports—and almost 80 per cent of Québec exports) retain their rights in these interior seas until 1985.

This Canadian legislation came a little late, and some countries accepted it all the more willingly because they were no longer catching enough to make fishing profitable in these waters, given the capacity of their modern industrial fishing vessels. In fact, the only real effect was to push the foreign armada out of these territories, to twelve nautical miles off the entrances to the Strait of Belle-Isle and the Cabot Strait, where in the winter and spring they caught the fish migrating to the Gulf waters, and in the autumn those leaving this biological pump to escape the ice.

In the view of the fishermen, the position Canada took at the International Convention on the Law of the Sea, at Caracas last spring, makes much more sense. It aims to push the territorial limit to two hundred miles from the coast, which means that almost the entire continental shelf would fall under Canadian jurisdiction. . . . A Vessel Surveillance Report in the 1 November 1973, issue of *The Sou'Wester* (a bimonthly published in Yarmouth that defines itself as "the voice of the fishing industry of the Atlantic provinces") gives some idea of the size of the foreign fishing effort near our coasts:

During a ten-day surface surveillance, from 1 to 10 October, in the 52nd region—one of the zones established by the

International Commission for the Northwest Atlantic Fisheries (ICNAF), a United Nations agency, for setting quotas of takes by species and by country—which extends to five degrees of longitude southwest of Cape Cod, ships identified, aside from Canadian and American ones, included twenty vessels from West Germany, seventeen from East Germany, fifteen from the U.S.S.R., thirty Spanish trawlers, ten Japanese ships, five Bulgarian ships, and two French ships.

On 16 October, during an aerial survey conducted north and west of Nova Scotia, twenty-five foreign ships were observed, including one American south of Cross Island, two Spanish north of Scatarie Island, ten Spanish south of Saint-Pierre and Miquelon, two Spanish and one Soviet south of Cape Canso, and seven West German sixty miles north of Sable Island.

The same day, the coast-guard ship Chebucto observed twenty-seven Polish trawlers and two factory ships in the north part of Georges Bank, as well as a number of Spanish, Bulgarian, and German ships.

Giovanni Caboto, the Genoese navigator and contemporary of Christopher Columbus, was the first to officially report on the prodigious fertility of the Gulf waters. Before him, Scandinavian, Flemish, Basque, and Breton fishermen were already visiting Newfoundland's Grand Banks but, as good fishermen are wont to do, they did not breathe a word of the origin of their almost miraculous catches.

The old people of the Magdalen Islands keep as a precious memory the images passed on to them by their grandparents of bays that filled each spring with Grand Banks schooners, at a time when all fishing was done with lines. From each ship cast off a number of small dories set out with flags and sails of the same colour as those of the ship to which they belonged; from these fishermen caught herring to bait the hooks on the cod lines. In spite of their number, they could do no great damage to the fish populations, and even the advent of the gillnet and the seine did no great harm, since the ships were sail-powered and the work was performed by hand. It was the mechanization of all of these activities, up to today's gigantism, that tolled the knell for a number of species by allowing excessive takes.

Another factor impeding stock recovery is pollution of the oceans, which is reaching such alarming proportions that the Canadian government's major argument for increasing its territorial waters to two hundred miles from its coasts was environmental. Hydrocarbons alter the gaseous exchange between the ocean and the atmosphere. Oil companies use the oceans as garbage cans and flush their tankers on the high seas; the occasional shipwreck is even more serious. All classes of ships release their wastewater and trash into the ocean every day. The Americans have even deposited their nuclear waste and poison gas considered too toxic to keep on land, even though it is known that the marine abysses contain different forms of life and are swept by powerful currents.

As well as this direct pollution of the oceans, there is also telluric—earth-based—pollution, due to run-off from our polluted watercourses and the settling of dust from our polluted atmosphere, which accounts to about three-fourths of ocean pollution, according to Canadian Hydrography Service researchers. The great sewer of North American civilization, as many ecologists today call the St. Lawrence River, empties into the Gulf, and it is easy to understand why salmon shun these filthy waters and no longer run up rivers in which they once abounded—rivers now also polluted by various industrial installations.

In addition to these consequences, which are inherent to a certain notion we have of progress, human manipulation of the natural environment has not always had beneficial effects. For instance, construction of the Canso causeway in 1955 closed the strait that separated Cape Breton Island from Nova Scotia (except for a swing bridge to permit passage of ships). The powerful current that swept into this mile-long narrow strait played an important role in the migration of fish and in oxygenation and plankton supply for part of the Gulf waters.

...

Under these circumstances, the fishing industry finds itself in a weak position. In Newfoundland, the main fish-producing province, Frank Moores's government has deemed the situation serious enough to name the ex-Minister of Finance and cabinet heavyweight John C. Crosbie to the fisheries portfolio. In normal times, this would be considered more a demotion than a promotion; today, however, the challenge is great: to save the principal industry of the province! Crosbie has warned that the territorial limit must be extended to two hundred miles from the coast within the next year or it will be too late.

Fishermen often hear talk of these sudden, inexorable deadlines. As scientists in their own way (one must not underestimate, as certain biologists tend to do, the very accurate and complete knowledge they have of the marine environment), the fishermen know that the abundance of species corresponds to cycles that result in good and bad years. They also know that species cannot repopulate without a certain number of individuals, below which they are irremediably headed for extinction.

The redfish, which has been relentlessly fished for a number of years in the waters of the Gulf by a good five dozen trawlers each of which can catch 125 tonnes per outing, are approaching this critical stage. All the fishermen agree that if the government does not ban fishing for at least the two months of the "rave" (spawning season) starting this spring, this species will disappear for a long time, especially since redfish do not reach maturity until between eleven and fifteen years of age.

Fishermen understand even less why the companies rush to pursue the unfortunate redfish, since they know that there are inventories in cold storage in Halifax and Gloucester amounting to tens of millions of pounds! At first they thought that it was a tactic to raise the retail price, but no: the market had actually collapsed... And the federal government had to intervene last autumn to lower the inventories: it bought redfish and canned it to be sent to countries suffering from famine as part of its foreign aid programme.

...

As for the small inshore fisherman, celebrated by poets, he cannot hear technocratic terms like production rationalization or concentration of technical resources without a shiver of anxiety, since he knows that these wise words in fact signal the condemnation of all the fishing centres that the government considers unprofitable—more precisely, of his little harbour, which has the double advantage of being near both his home and his fishing grounds...

Last summer, tired of being considered almost nonentities, if not a species on the way to extinction, the small inshore fishermen of the Gaspé took up their guns to fire on the Québec trawlers that had come to sweep the ocean floor so close to the coast that they were wreaking havoc on the traps and carrying off long lines and gillnets. As of last December, the Québec Fisheries Department still had not come up with a solution to this pressing problem, in spite, said the irritated fishermen, of a centuries-old maritime tradition that gave priority to the least well equipped, and according to which the sailing ship has priority over the steamship, and fishermen working with fixed gear (traps, nets, lines, etc.) have priority over trawlers, which can easily pass around their fishing territory as long as it is adequately marked.

Each fisherman has his problems, but there's nothing like good fishing to help him forget them. When, by chance, a full load is hoisted up, one which it takes two turns at the gilson to board, faces light up. With pleasure, fishermen then kneel on the bridge to gut, one by one, the innumerable cod that have flooded it—and feel not the slightest disgust, but only joy, to still find themselves there, some hours later, in viscera and pink livers up to their hipwaders, as they slide on their knees in the thick, viscous waves moving and shifting like the ocean—while, above, crowds of hungry seagulls and herring gulls cry and squabble over the tiniest bit of tripe thrown overboard.*

---

* Reproduced with the kind permission of Maclean-Hunter.

7

An Industry in
Long-Term Intensive Care

THE 1970S, MARKED by the implementation of new laws and strict catch quotas per species and fishing zone, added a new, doleful refrain to the traditional litany of fishermen. "If there are fish, there's no market, and if there's a market there's no fish" was now followed by "And when there are fish and a market, my hands are tied by regulations".

Of course, things had to be regulated to avoid an irreparable catastrophe, the dreaded day when the last cod-fish would be pulled from the ocean. By 1975, it was clear that the banning of foreign trawlers from the Gulf of St. Lawrence and the Bay of Fundy had not magically brought back the fish; on the contrary, Canadians were proving to be as effective at pillaging as the foreigners. Like them, they were at the mercy "of other, more powerful forces than the wind, the tides, and the ice", Roméo Leblanc, then minister of state for Fisheries, said in a speech before the Magdalen Islands Chamber of Commerce in June, 1976.

"Why, exactly, has it become so difficult for the fisherman to earn a livelihood?" Leblanc asked. And he gave this answer:" Those who are responsible, even if they don't know it, are the fishermen themselves. Fishing techniques have evolved more in the last thirty years than in the last thirty centuries, in Canada as well. Our efficiency is at least twice as high as that of all other countries that operate in the northwest Atlantic. The fish have decreased in number mainly because of foreign fishing fleets, for, even if they are less effective, their size ensures them ten times the tonnage of our fleet. But, in many cases, Canadians and Canadians alone are responsible for the exhaustion of stocks. If you want to look at a sector that falls exclusively under Canada's jurisdiction, a sector in which foreign ships have completely disappeared and which, nevertheless, has falling stocks, just look around us. It is the Gulf of St. Lawrence. . . . The problems that are caused by the foreign fleets are repeated on the national level."

This was a thinly veiled allusion to the problems that Leblanc anticipated with the two-hundred-mile exclusive economic zone. And on that very day, it was clearn that the E.E.Z. would not be the hoped-for panacea.

The Convention on the Law of the Sea, while giving the nod in principle to two-hundred-mile exclusive economic zones for coastal states, refused to ratify the "and farther" qualifier proposed by Canada. The northern cod thus escaped Canadian control during its winter migration. As well, those gullible enough to believe that the two-hundred-mile zone would give Canadian fishermen exclusive access, as they had in the Gulf of St. Lawrence and the Bay of Fundy, were quite disappointed: it was not exclusive access, in fact, but only exclusive management, since, as was repeated often and in a very humanitarian tone by Roméo Leblanc, Canada did not want starve the other countries of the world.

In fact, there were negotiations with each of the ICNAF countries throughout the duration of the Convention on the Law of the Sea, leading to bilateral agreements which took into account the historical rights of the countries that had long been fishing on the banks of the northwest Atlantic. Some quotas were adjusted —so many capelin against so many redfish, so many mackerel against so many shrimp, grenadier at will, and so on— so as to free certain cod stocks for the Canadian trawlers, but this was well below the expectations of those in the fishing industry who, lured by the promise of new abundance, had considerably increased their catching and processing capacities.

"We have imposed permit restrictions with regard to almost all Canadian fisheries", Mr. Leblanc announced in his speech before the Magdalen Islands Chamber of Commerce. "With the two-hundred-mile limit, we will have more effective surveillance of foreign fleets. We will be able to tell them what, when, and how much to fish. We will have the power to limit foreign ships to certain zones, make them submit reports, grant and suspend permits as needed, seize ships for infractions, and impose fines and penalties in our own courts."

If Canada did not manage to get more from these negotiations, it was because international maritime law requires the sharing of fishing resources in "excess of needs"—and Canadians are, alas, not great consumers of fish.

Perhaps fish has retained its connotation of a food of penance, or perhaps many people still remember childhood days when they blocked their noses and swallowed spoonfuls of codliver oil in the winter months. For whatever reason, in the 1970s Canadians consumed only about seven and a half kilos of fish per capita each year. Even in the 1980s, with the intense publicity seafood products received, the rise of physical-fitness fads, and the influx of immigrants from fish-consuming countries, the rate of fish consumption did not rise much. It is nowhere near that of Spain, Portugal, Britain, Japan, or other Asian nations, whose citizens consume four, five, six, and even ten times more fish, mollusks, and shellfish than we do. Under these circumstances, it is difficult to claim to the rest of the world that we have no fish in excess of our needs to share with other countries.

Obviously, Canada could have fished and then sold its catch to consuming countries. (It in fact does this for a certain number of species, which undergo basic processing here and are shipped elsewhere [e.g., snow crabs to Japan], or are sold over the board onto the factory ships of other countries [herring and mackerel to the Russians].) This was particularly feasible since there existed (and still exists) a bewildering processing overcapacity for our seafood products, which meant that in the best fishing years, the plants on the Atlantic coast worked on average to only 50 per cent of capacity. More raw material would certainly have been welcome at these companies, even for the most rudimentary processing: beheading, gutting, freezing.

But there were two major obstacles: the foreign fleets already had numerous freezer-trawlers and factory ships, and
Canada had a reputation of producing very low-quality fish
until the mid-1980s, when vigorous efforts were made to improve it. The Boston Blue Sheet, which lists North American
market prices for fish, quoted Canadian cod at a much lower
price than cod from Iceland and Norway, which was handled
much more carefully right from the ship up to the
consumer's table.

During the 1970s, the rule in Canada was still to prong the
fish into and out of the hold, without looking where the tines
pierced the fish, whether in the head or in the stomach; this
resulted in ugly lesions and blood stains in the fillets. Although pronging was perhaps acceptable when the fish was
salted, because the salt immediately cauterized the wounds,
it was not acceptable for other types of preservation, especially blocks and frozen fillets—not to mention the fresh-cod
market!

For all of these reasons, the Canadian industry was not
ready to play its role fully when the two-hundred-mile zone
was proclaimed, and by the time it raised the standard of its
product to match that of Iceland and Japan, it was too late.
When the new, ultra-modern plants constructed or updated
at great cost in the Gaspé, the Magdalen Islands, Nova
Scotia, New Brunswick, and Newfoundland opened their
doors, some people were already wondering whether there
would really be enough fish for them to process. But, since
the quality of Canadian fish had improved, they sometimes
received catches from foreign trawlers, whose owners used
this as leverage with the competent authorities of Fisheries
and Oceans Canada to renegotiate upward their allocation of
various species in the two-hundred-mile economic zone.
Thus, fish caught by Soviet trawlers before Glasnost and
processed at the Newport plant in the Gaspé ended up, called
Mac-something, in the mouths of American customers of the
famous chain.

In the meantime, even before the territorial waters were extended to two hundred miles from its shores, the fishing in-

dustry in the Atlantic region was in a major crisis because of the lack of fish. The intensive pillage of the Gulf had made 1973 "the most profitable year for many sectors of the industry", according to an Environment Canada, Fisheries and Oceans, document dated May, 1976, and entitled *Canadian Policy for the Commercial Fishery". However, it didn't last : "large sectors of the industry that were subject to chronic difficulties almost went bankrupt during the last months of 1974" and, in fact, the entire structure was threatening to crumble.*

On the Atlantic coast, the fishery employed about 47,000 fiserhmen and about 20,000 people in fish processing and marketing. It reported almost $700 million in revenue nationally (the dollar was worth about $3.60 in 1992 dollars), half of this sum representing the wholesale value of exports, the other half the retail value of products sold in Canada. This was not in itself a very large chunk of the Canadian economy, but still more than just a drop in the ocean.

At the regional level, however, fishing was crucially important. Dependence on commercial fisheries and connected industries was (and still is) extremely high in all parts of the Atlantic coast: about 75 per cent of all communities participate in the fishery, and about 20 per cent of them, comprising a total of 250,000 people, have no source of income other than that generated by the fishery. In Newfoundland, 15 per cent of all labour worked directly in the fishery and fish processing in the mid-1970s.

In order to avoid plunging the entire Atlantic region into a depression, the federal government provided large grants both to fishermen, who received a few cents per pound of high-quality groundfish landed, and to the industry, which also received a few cents per pound of high-quality frozen fillet or block produced. Over all, this aid amounted to $130 million (at dollar value in respective years) spread over 1974, 1975, and 1976.

The fact that this special aid was added to annual statutory expenditures of almost $200 million (dollar value of the mid-seventies) already dedicated by the federal and provincial administrations to the commercial fishery reveals not only the true scope of the crisis, but also one of the underlying causes and endemic ills of the Canadian fisheries: poor management of the entire industry. In the 1970s, it required no less than a half-billion 1992 dollars in various subsidies every year to function! And this figure doesn't include the salaries of an exponentially expanding public service to administer everything at both levels of government.

In government archives, there are probably more reports, summaries, policy statements, working documents, statistics, analyses, task-force reports, directories, and other papers on the fisheries than cod that will be caught this year. "You might think that the top priority of fisheries management is to prop up the pulp-and-paper industry" was the caustic comment of one fisherman.

The sad thing is that, since 1920, all the reports and professions of noble intentions have said just about the same thing. Indeed, the 1928 Report of the Royal Commission on the Québec and Maritime Fisheries sought to find permanent solutions to the fisheries problem, or "to suggest, at least, methods of permanent relief, rather than . . . temporary palliatives". Nevertheless, it conceded that, in spite of exhaustive studies done in the past, a good number of these questions did not yet have permanent solutions, and admitted, "The difficulties and disabilities are so many, so varied, and so intricate, that their complete and final removal will require from the department patient and perhaps prolonged endeavour."

Indeed. The 1976 document *Canadian Policy for the Commercial Fishery* concurred, and the title of the Kirby Report, issued six years later, *Navigating Troubled Waters*, confirmed it yet again.

If a new document were published today, it would no doubt say just about the same thing. The Kirby Report was honest enough to recognize this, commenting, with an almost audible sigh, about the problems that had been analyzed in 1928, "Despite the fact that the problem was identified at least 54 years ago, it is distressing to note that the conclusions of this Task Force are substantially similar to those of the Royal Commission and show that very little has been done to attack this basic problem of the industry." And yet it dared to reiterate, without the slightest fear of ridicule, the same absolutely unarguable and reassuring truisms that the fishermen who had been weathering the crisis for twenty years had already read in *Canadian Policy for the Commercial Fishery:*

> The Canadian fishing industry has good potential for expansion. It is situated close to fishing territories capable of becoming the most productive in the world, and to very attractive food-consumption markets. The extension of the national territorial jurisdiction for the fisheries to at least two hundred miles from the coast can only improve the prospects for a well-established Canadian industry that processes its fish on shore. However, the materialization of these prospects requires a new direction in management policy and development of the fisheries.*

This document did, however, correctly identify the grotesque errors of the past:

> The federal government, which has the task of preserving and regulating access to the fishery resource and encouraging expansion of the industry, must also study the social problems resulting from excessive dependence on the fishery in certain regions. Under these circumstances, emergency measures may be confused with true fishery development and result in the creation of short-term programmes that are in conflict with long-term objectives. For example, the government has supported construction of new processing plants (in the name of contributing to industrial progress) and imposed restric-

---

* Compare with the Kirby Report, *Navigating Troubled Waters : A New Policy for the Atlantic Fishery*, p. 9: "The fishery confronts us with a troubling paradox. On one doorstep, we have one of the world's great natural fisheries resource bases....On another doorstep is the United States, a major and accessible market for fish....The purpose of this Report is to try to set a course for everyone involved in the fishery....a course that will enable them to navigate successfully the troubled waters of the Atlantic fishery."

tions on the take (in the name of conservation) in the same place at the same time."

However, this admission did not prevent Leblanc or, even less, his successor at Fisheries and Oceans, Pierre DeBané (for political reasons this time), from setting up the federally financed Cartier Fishery plants at various locations in the Gaspé with the single goal of competing with the Pêcheurs Unis plants financed by Québec, even though the fish allocations were barely enough to keep the latter going.

But let's return to the 1976 *Canadian Policy for the Commercial Fishery*. After noting that in order to remedy the crisis, the minister of state for fisheries of the time, Mr. Leblanc, had asked for the most complete study of the fishing industry since the war, and would base his actions on the study's recommendations, the document frankly admitted that with regard to stock management, the Canadian government's interventions had proven not very judicious.

"Up to the present", it stated, with the nebulous discretion of official texts trying to avoid saying anything unpleasant, "exploitation of the fishery resources has aimed, when necessary, to ensure the maximum sustainable biological yield. This measure corresponds poorly, if at all, to the best combination of benefits for humans, because, in fact, in certain cases it does not even protect the relationship between fish populations."

In plain English, this means that the government was tolerating overfishing of certain species at levels such that their natural predators did not have enough to eat and had to look elsewhere. The new fisheries policy was aimed at ending this practice—everyone likes to be virtuous—stating forthrightly that in the future,

> ...the principle directive for fisheries management will no longer be to push the biological yield to the maximum, but to encourage a better use of the society's resources (manpower and capital as well as fish populations). Fundamental decisions on management of the resource and on expansion of the industry and the business are to be taken jointly by the industry and the government.

Of course, the aim of this policy was to create a strong and stable industry that ensures a satisfactory standard of living for all participants. However, there is quite a way from the cup to the lips. As much to satisfy the demands of the industry, which wanted its equipment to be profitable, as to see to the "social welfare" aspect and create jobs, the authorities charged with fixing the TAC (total allowable catch) for the various zones and species, also sensitive to political winds, had once again started to allow fish catches, year after year, in numbers beyond the scientists' recommendations.

To make matters worse, scientists had grossly overestimated the cod populations—in particular, the northern cod stock.

8

The Cape Freels on Patrol

AT FIRST THEY COULD BE FOUND only by radar, and one had to be almost on top of them to see them emerging from the fog: enormous dark masses labouring and weaving as they towed their trawls in the swells of the Grand Banks. Some of them were so large that they dwarfed the *Cape Freels*, the Canadian coast-guard frigate (since then lost at sea) that carried us. But with her two cannons, she impressed the trawlers of the international fleets quite a bit!

It was 1975. I spent fourteen days on the ocean with a T.V. crew from Radio-Canada's *Le 60* to film the ships that were pillaging our resources. The weather was horrible as we patrolled the northern part of the Grand Banks, almost right up to the Flemish Cap. We were looking for Soviet units, of which we had seen only two or three of the some forty that had been detected fishing in the area: huge rusting ships, with tired hulls, that rolled to port and starboard, pitched and yawed in the immense swells, and emerged, drooling foam from the scuppers. They looked like they were barely moving despite the black smoke belching from their stacks, so hard were they working to pull their huge trawl at the end of tightly stretched cables that plunged into the grey waves from the top of the aft beam.

I had already seen these huge ships moored in St. John's harbour, with their sailors, fishermen, and women workers leaning over the rails and waving to passersby on the docks. I imagined the women working in the plant down below, tossed about by the waves, their chapped hands beheading, gutting, and freezing or otherwise preserving the fish. Besides the guts and the starfish, the Soviets seemed to throw little back into the ocean. The gulls that rushed to the stern of the ship every time they lifted the trawl, circling with their raucous cries while the catch was sorted, stayed hungry. By now, they might have known that the ships flying the red flag with the hammer and the sickle (in the open sea, perhaps a hook would have been more appropriate) were inordinately stingy.

The swell was too high to board the Soviet ships. On the *Cape Freels*, Captain Blackwood hoisted some flags to ask the Soviet captain to open radio communication. A Fisheries Department inspector asked some questions about the catch, checking off the answers on various forms, then the frigate hoisted another series of flags on a port halyard—to say goodbye and wish them good fishing, the captain told me—and the *Cape Freels* veered off and ploughed through the waves in search of other units of the fleet.

A few days later, near the Whale Deep, in the southern Grand Banks, we met the Spanish fleet: a swarm of fireflies on the radar screen, which lit up each time the antenna beam swept the zone. It was only when the *Cape Freels* was within a few knots that their silhouettes emerged from the waves. From closer, with binoculars, we could make out their names, painted in white letters on the grey hulls: usually *Santa* something, and, beneath, their home port, Vigo. These were also large ships, at least two hundred feet long, dominated by high, arching beams on the poop deck, from the summit of which the trawl cables disappeared into the ocean.

"Pair trawlers", Captain Blackwood informed me, after he asked the helmsman to get closer to one trawler. (The Spanish call them *parea*.) The fog was so thick that the other ship was visible only on the radar screen. I imagined the immense trawl sweeping the deeps between the two ships. "Each ship takes a turn lifting the trawl", Captain Blackwood told me. "It wreaks havoc on the fish."

The swell was still too high, and dusk was falling. We put the inspection off to the next day. During the evening watch, the wind turned to the northwest, blowing away the fog. Under a star-studded sky appeared a garland of small lights, sprinkled here and there, dancing on the ocean, rising and falling with the swells, dotting the inky waves all the way to the horizon: this was the entire Spanish fleet, with perhaps some Portuguese ships as well, fishing tirelessly through the night. Sometimes, one of the luminous dots shone more brightly as they lit the fishing deck to hoist the trawl.

On the radio, mixed with the crackling, whistling static, we heard the captains talking. I didn't understand what they were saying (only an experienced ear can understand even one's *native* tongue on these apparatuses), but I recognized the general tone of the conversations, which I had heard between draggers from Port-aux-Basques, Sydney, Lunenburg, and Souris, during my own helm watches on long, monotonous nocturnal trawl runs: the weary voices of men fighting sleep, whose silence was sometimes more eloquent than their words.

The next morning, by the time the siren woke me, the Fisheries Department officers had returned from their inspection tour. From the boat, which had already been hoisted on board by the cathead, nice flounder and big halibut were unloaded, the largest of which must have weighed more than a hundred pounds. The cook and the sailors gutted, filleted, and cut them up for dinner. There were also some good-sized cod that the Spanish captain had given to the boat pilot from Newfoundland, no doubt noticing his eyes light up when he saw their catch. For all Newfoundlanders, the sea is a garden and cod the most succulent of its fruits.

"We could have brought back ten times more halibut and flounder", the pilot told me as he filleted his cod on the aft deck of the *Cape Freels*. "A fishing boat could make a fortune just going from one Spanish ship to another and picking up what they throw away. They only keep cod, which they salt on board. *Bacalao*, nothing else." The twinkle in his eye told me that he didn't think that they were entirely mistaken—or, at least, that he appreciated their good taste. "It's because they still salt on board", he explained. "And everyone knows that flatfish don't salt well."

All day, the *Cape Freels* went from one ship to another, opening dialogue with the international language of flags, following up on the radio. Then the boat was lowered into the water, and the ICNAF officers and a Fisheries Department biologist boarded the trawler to inspect the ship's log, the catch and discard reports, the mesh of the nets, the average size of the catches, and so on. If they found infractions, they could neither impound nor arrest, but simply report them to ICNAF. The Commission would advise the ship's country, to which it would then fall to take the appropriate sanctions against the captain.

The inspectors sometimes returned from foreign trawlers bitterly grumbling that their hands were tied by international protocols and looking forward to the day when Canada would extend its jurisdiction to two hundred miles. There were indeed infractions, especially with regard to mesh size—of course, not in the nets the draggers winched up, full of fish, while the officers were on board, since the ships had passed the word among them that a Canadian patrol vessel was on the prowl and had put away their small-mesh trawls, but in those that the inspectors saw in the stores, which had obviously not been brought from the other end of the Atlantic just to lie idle.

"I'd bet my life that the first trawler we inspected this morning has already put its small-mesh lining back on its trawl, because they know were not coming back," muttered one of the officers at the end of the afternoon. "With that thing, even the sardines won't get away!"

Our team wanted to film on board one of these trawlers, but we required permission from the captain. When one finally agreed, the inspectors then objected, saying that the seas had swelled and ferrying personnel and equipment across might be dangerous. I thus had to do away with my stand-up report in cod up to my knees, for which I'd brought my hipwaders and oilskins, and satisfy myself with talking to the camera with a ship from the foreign fleet in the background. This was a much less striking image, since all ships tend to look small in the distance against the vastness of the ocean.

On the days that followed days, as we approached the Cabot Strait, we saw some Portuguese trawlers on the Green Bank and the Saint-Pierre Bank, but the *Cape Freels's* orders did not include this zone, nor the banks farther south—Artimon, Banquereau, Le Hone, Canso, Georges, and so on—where, Captain Blackwood told me, there were large concentrations of Polish and German ships. It was only when we approached Cape Race that we finally saw a Canadian vessel: a small, twenty-metre side-trawler, beside which the *Cape Freels* suddenly looked like a National Marine frigate.

That was perhaps the most striking image of the fourteen days at sea.

9

Prey for the Shadow

THE KIRBY REPORT, CALLED *Navigating Troubled Waters* and subtitled *A New Policy for the Atlantic Fisheries*, is truly the Cadillac of Canadian policy statements on the fisheries. Its cover features a grainy photograph of three fishermen taken from the back as they pull up a seine, not on a large industrial ship but on a modest little Cape-Islander. The three objectives the government wanted Senator Michael J.L.

Kirby's Atlantic Fisheries Task Force to examine were how to build an economically viable fishing industry, how to fulfil the governments social role as a provider of employment, and how—by God!—to keep the fishery fiercely Canadian. So Canadian, in fact, that the task force had no *French* Canadian among its twelve members.

However, although it vibrated with Canadian chauvinism,* especially in the chapters dealing with international issues and the harvesting of the northern cod, the Task Force did not find it necessary to analyze or trace the cause of this penchant in a section entitled "The Role of Ideology", where it only justified its politico-economic bent and, notably, where it "discounted much of the free enterprise rhetoric as just that—rhetoric".

This does not mean that the Task Force did not take account of the point of view of industry representatives. Nor was it incorrect when it wrote that it "frankly...does not see what this phrase ['free enterprise system'] means in the context of the Atlantic fishing industry", in which, at the slightest sign of rough seas, even owners most hostile to government interventionism were holding out their hands to the public treasury—knowing very well that these alms would not be refused since they were the only employers in fishing communities and that without such largess, social chaos would ensue.

The Task Force certainly showed its true colours in this matter. But in the same way that it analyzed and demonstrated its preferences with regard to political economics, it might have, and even should have, done the same regarding its Canadian chauvinism, especially because these types of documents are read in foreign countries and are sometimes confused with the country's official policy, which can result in annoying quid pro quos. We will return to this point later on.

---

* The Kirby Report strongly recommended abrogation of the 1928 federal-provincial agreement giving Québec exclusive jurisdiction over its inshore fishery.

Still and all, the Kirby Report constitutes the most complete and probing attempt to resolve the internal antagonisms (inshore fishermen versus offshore fishermen, plant workers versus producers, small business versus big business) that were causing an endemic condition of sand in the gears of the Canadian fishing industry—antagonisms that had brought it practically to bankruptcy's doorstep when the Department of Fisheries and Oceans ordered the study, in 1981.

The crisis that had already justified the injection of $130 million in various grants from 1974 to 1976 had thereafter entered a different stage, mainly because of two factors. First, there was an increase in catching and processing capacities, the result of hopes based on the extension of Canada's exclusive fishing zone to two hundred miles from the coast. Second, there was the collapse of the Gulf redfish stocks (with landings falling from 107,000 tonnes in 1973 to 6,400 tonnes in 1977, reproducing over a five-year period the appalling plunge in Canadian cod catches, which had gone from 1,900,000 tonnes in 1968 to 480,000 tonnes in 1972).

Meanwhile, cod catches increased slightly, surpassing 600,000 tonnes in 1980 and 1981, giving rise to the falsest of hopes. The fisheries are like dominoes: when one falls, the others feel the effects. Deprived of their source of redfish, which constituted 70 per cent of their take, the large Gulf trawlers asked for and received replacement quotas of cod, which seemed by then to be on the rebound. This forced a reallocation of cod quotas assigned in the Gulf to trawlers based outside the area and the transfer of these permits to other fishing zones, that is, those situated east and northeast of Newfoundland and extending two hundred miles from the coast. The quotas for cod in the recovering stocks of the Grand Banks and Labrador (management zone 2J3KL) could not, in their turn, be granted to the ex-redfish trawlers from outside the Gulf unless allocations for the Newfoundland inshore fishermen and, of course, foreign fleets were re-assessed.

Very fortunately, the opening of new fisheries, like that for shrimp on banks that had not yet been exploited, and for snow crab, up to then called *chancre* by Acadian fishermen and thrown back into the water, enabled many offshore fishermen to adapt—and to prosper, because of the abundance of the resource—by harvesting these shellfish.

This reallocation of catches, called the Management Plan for Atlantic Groundfish, also had to take into account the proximity of processing plants, for which adequate supply raised the question of the social role of the industry in remote communities. To complicate the problem, the number of plants had grown 35 per cent between 1977 and 1981, from 519 to 700. Each one of them was expecting a miraculous fish harvest due to the extension of the Canadian zone to two hundred miles.

There was a pressing need to restructure the entire industry right up to the marketing phase, since Canadian cod did not occupy a very attractive niche on the American market. Of inferior quality to Iceland's product, which monopolized the white-tablecloth and fast-food restaurant sectors, it was usually bought in the "captive-food" (plant cafeterias, school cafeterias, the military, hospitals, prisons) and retail sectors. In these sectors, supply already exceeded demand (what would happen when the bonanza of the economic zone hit?) and meats, as always, offered tough competition to groundfish as a source of food protein. The average American, in fact, consumes 105.8 kilos of meat per year (72.4 kilos of red meat and 27.6 kilos of fowl), but only 1.8 kilos of groundfish and 4 kilos of other fish, mollusks, and shellfish.

But the law of scale, in which tiny index variations can have immense repercussions on the whole, made Michael Kirby's Task Force optimistic. If Americans' protein-consumption habits could be modified by just 0.1 per cent per year over a period of five years, the Task Force reasoned, this would produce an increased demand for groundfish that would absorb all of the anticipated increase in catch in Atlantic Canada, estimated at no less than 50 per cent. This was the expected fruit of sound Canadian management of cod in its economic zone.

On the marketing side, all that was needed was for each and every American to eat one more pound of fish per year—just a few bites, really!—over five years, and the means for obtaining these extra mouthfuls existed. Others—fowl producers, milk-product producers, etc.—had demonstrated the effectiveness of similar nutritional motivational campaigns: advertising was the answer. The cost of triggering the hoped-for Pavlovian reflex could even be measured: it was estimated that it would take between six and ten million dollars to make Americans salivate satisfactorily before a serving of cod.

In nine months, with the cooperation of all interested parties, the Kirby Task Force accomplished the titanic task of investigating all components of the problem: the resource, harvesting, processing, marketing, and the creation, after repeated consultation with fishermen, plant workers, and industrialists, of a coherent fisheries policy that could ensure, if not prosperity, at least an acceptable standard of living for everyone.

There is one aspect of the issue that does not seem to have been examined as deeply as the others, even though it was the very foundation of the edifice: the state of the resource itself. In this regard, it appears today that the Task Force accepted the evaluations of Canadian scientists too easily, even though they were imbued with a delirious optimism.

Did the Task Force succumb, as so many have done so often, to the blind faith which we seem to have in scientific truth— and do so all the more willingly because the oracle's predictions were exactly what they wanted to hear? In its public hearings, the Task Force should have heeded the few discordant warnings from old, skeptical fishermen (who had only the qualifications of long experience of life and of the sea, it is true, with which to oppose the calculations of the biometricists), but it is evident that it turned a deaf ear.

In 1982, scientific word had it that the cod stocks, over-exploited for twenty years and having reached their lowest catch level in a century only a few years earlier, were incredibly resilient and in full recovery. The slight rise in landings in 1980 and

1981 for all cod populations was hard proof, but this was just the beginning, said the biometricists. The northern cod—the brave beast!—was registering such an increase in biomass that, the experts predicted, the TAC would increase by at least 170,000 tonnes, or 75 per cent, between 1982 and 1987, which would bring the Canadian quota up to at least 380,000 tonnes for 1987 for zone 2J3KL.

The members of the Kirby Task Force were so euphoric that they made up a little limerick, excerpted at the beginning of chapter 12 of *Navigating Troubled Waters*, which dealt with exploitation of the northern-cod stock:

The cod of 2J, 3KL
Produces excitement pell-mell,
It's a fast-growing stock,
Which all want to dock
Who will get it? Well, we're here to tell.

There was certainly no lack of strong Canadian pride in this presumptuous ditty; wasn't it in fact since Canada was exclusively managing this stock, considered moribund just yesterday, that it was demonstrating such vitality? Of course, it may also have been the cod themselves, expressing by their extraordinary demographic ardour their gratitude toward their new country, the chosen haven for so many immigrants, as we know....

For whatever reason, it seemed obvious that Canada had something to do with the recovery, and the Kirby Report wasn't coy, making several firm recommendations whose aim was to guarantee that Canadians enjoyed a higher-priority, if not exclusive, access to this abundance. "Allocation of the increase in the northern cod stock will cause controversy, the report stated, "yet it represents the best remaining opportunity to achieve better income for fishermen and greater utilization of processing capacity..." It was also recommended in chapter 9 that allocations attributed to foreign fleets be minimized.

The Kirby Task Force, as we can see, had made this prediction of abundant cod in 2J3KL, if not the cornerstone, then at least the midship beam of its fishery policy. In fact, this abundance did not exist—not at the level predicted, at any rate. The biometricists were grossly mistaken, as they would later discover. A simple glance at the curve of northern cod catches, which fell from almost 800,000 tonnes to less than 100,000 tonnes between 1968 and 1978, should have tempered enthusiasm, dissipated the mirage, shown the aberration. But they chose to look only at the small segment of the chart in which catches rose, without taking into account the vertiginous plunge they had previously taken.

It might also have come to mind that, since cod eggs are so vulnerable that only one or two out of several million escape a horde of predators and become a mature fish, the cod were not likely to breed like rabbits. But, no! The optimism was such that the few research data indicating a downward trend were considered aberrations. Ironically, the section of the Kirby Report that immediately follows the one dealing with the phenomenal growth of the northern cod stock, which deals with conflicts between inshore fishermen and offshore fishermen, is entitled "Myths and Realities".

However, carried away by the illusion of a population explosion among northern cod, the Kirby Report, like the Book of Allah, detailed everything, down to the last cod tail. It predicted which Scandinavian-type gillnetters would be used to fish the northern cod; it mentioned that the occasional foreign trawler would be called in to catch so many fish in such and such a zone to supply a Canadian plant in the foul-weather seasons when ships of lesser tonnage could not go out. It made provisions for a safety valve of fifty thousand tonnes of cod fished in the summer and frozen, which would enable the processing plants, equipped with plate freezers, to function twelve months a year. It recommended dockside catch-inspection programmes to guarantee quality—an excellent idea, by the way—and so on. Everything was in place for the curtain to rise: the scene was set, the script written, the lights lit. The only thing missing was the star of the show: *Gadus morhua.*

If I talked above about what seemed to me to be Canadian chauvinism in the report of the Task Force on the Atlantic Fisheries, it is because when I reread it, having returned from a tour of Europe with a Canadian fisheries delegation, I remembered a remark made by a senior official in the Spanish fisheries, who had protested, with sincere indignation, "Of course we use the TAC as a political weapon!"

This seemed very legitimate to him, even though he knew full well that overfishing by his country's ships on the edge of Canadian waters was, in fact, putting the northern cod stock in peril. Indeed, Enrique-Cesar Lopez Veiga, fisheries consultant for the Galicia independent region, the home port of the great trawlers, holds a doctoral degree in marine biology and had been involved in discussions on how the Grand Banks cod should be shared with Canada since the end of the 1970s. During our conversation, which took place at the parliament of Galicia, in Santiago de Compostella, Lopez Veiga also told us that the Spanish and the Galicians were very proud people and suggested that perhaps Canada's attitude toward them with regard to the fisheries had not always taken this into account.

The Kirby Report certainly must have ruffled this Iberian pride. In chapter 9, "International Issues", the report quoted a brief made to it by the Fisheries Association of Newfoundland and Labrador Ltd.: "The development of the Canadian resource for and by Canadians should be a paramount principle of fisheries policy"—a perfectly legitimate goal.

The recommendations that followed counselled allocating to foreign vessels fishing in the Canadian zone only "resources that are currently surplus to Canada's harvesting capacity (e.g., squid)", except when allocation of a certain quantity of non-surplus resources, like cod, would bring certain advantages to Canada, such as cooperation of foreign countries in protection of the resources or marketing of Canadian fisheries products. These "allocations...should be made after the fact—that is, in a subsequent year as a reward for satisfactory behaviour—rather than as an incentive."

There was nothing there, really, to wound even the most quixotic of sensibilities. It was the accompanying comments that were a bit more cutting, especially given the fundamental assumption of the Task Force that the northern cod stock was in phenomenal growth—to the point of making up limericks on the subject. This is equivalent to chanting "I've got it and you can't have it!" and thumbing one's nose to rub it in. In fact, since 1977, when the Canadian zone was extended to two hundred miles, foreign ships had seen their access to the cod in this sector progressively restricted, which gave rise to the accusation that a "surplus" had never been allocated by Canada in compliance with maritime law.

In this litigious context, with the threat of action before an international court, it is conceivable that the following text in the report seemed arrogant to foreign fishermen who, after all, had been visiting the Grand Banks since even before Canada existed. It must also have caused concern, for the embassies would have informed their superiors that Kirby had the ear of the prime minister of the time, Pierre Elliott Trudeau, with whom he was reputed to be good friends, and thus that there was good reason to think that his new policy would in fact become *the* policy in Canada with regard to the fishery.

Judge for yourself:

There is only one way to avoid the downward spiral that would be inevitable if pressures to allocate stocks to foreign fleets is not resisted. That is to pursue the Canadianization of fishing within the zone and, at the same time, to pursue market development and expansion of markets by conventional means rather than by way of allocations in return for market access. This is why we made Canadianization our third objective for fisheries policy and why we recommend an after-the-fact approach to foreign allocations rather than offering allocations before the fact in the hope that adequate marketing benefits might ensue.

The Law of the Sea Convention, in our view, does not require the allocation of resources to other countries in situations where to do so would have an adverse economic effect on the Canadian fishing industry. Indeed, it would be nonsense if international accords required nations to allocate to potential buyers fish that the buyers would then not have to purchase because they could catch it themselves.

Article 62 of the Law of the Sea Convention expressly provides that in giving other states access to its exclusive economic zone, the coastal state shall take into account all relevant factors, including the significance of the living resources of the area to the economy of the coastal state concerned. Article 61 provides that the coastal state may take the economic needs of coastal communities into account in determining appropriate conservation measures for the resources of the 200-mile zone.

We are therefore unable to support the view that because the fish is there it must be caught—if not by Canadians then by vessels from other countries. If we do not have a market for the species and it is genuinely surplus to our fishing economy, it should be allocated to other nations. Otherwise it should be stored in the cheapest manner possible, in the sea, until it can be profitably utilized.

On the issue of allocations of non-surplus resources in return for access to markets, our view that this practice should not be followed has widespread support within the industry. The allocation of non-surplus fish is expensive as well as unwise from a marketing point of view. One thousand tonnes of live cod yields about 20 person-years of direct employment in catching (by trawler) and processing. More labour is required for inshore harvesting. The marketed value of each 1000 tonnes of live cod is about $1 million.*

* Kirby Task Force Report, Chapter 9.

In 1981, Madrid had tried to negotiate with Ottawa a progressive decrease in Spanish fishing in the Canadian economic zone. "Give us ten years", proposed the Spanish, one of whose negotiators was none other than the above-mentioned Mr. Lopez Veiga. "Between now and then, we will redistribute our Grand Banks trawler fleet in other fishing zones around the world, and we will never bother Canada again." Tony Campbell, who was heading the Canadian negotiating team, felt that this was to both countries' advantage. The agreement came within inches of being signed and would in fact have been had not Canadian industrialists, their appetite piqued by scientists' promises of abundant northern cod, ferociously opposed it.

Kirby's *New Policy for the Atlantic Fisheries*, while sealing the fate of the negotiations, raised doubts about Canada's sincerity in the minds of the Spanish fishery managers—and, no doubt in other fishing countries as well. Had Canada negotiated in good faith? Or was it trying to gain time, as the Europeans claimed, while it developed a fleet of trawlers, a "catching power", which would later justify the allegation that there was in fact no surplus to share?

Since the ocean has no secrets except those it swallows, it was well known, among shipowners and in the fishery industry all over Europe, that the four largest fishing firms in Canada—National Sea Products, Fishery Products, H.B. Nickerson & Sons, and the Lake Group—as well as others had bought up, or were preparing to do so, from the Faroe Islands, Norway, and elsewhere, freezer-trawlers that were surplus in these countries now that fishing on the banks of Newfoundland was about to be closed to them.

Bitter over having been ridiculed, the Europeans—notably, the Spanish and Portuguese—soon decided to take outside the Canadian E.E.Z. what Canada was refusing them within it, all the while trumpeting far and wide the abundance of its fish stocks.

10

Foreign Overfishing
Beyond the Canadian E.E.Z.

IN 1981, WHEN CANADA was inches away from signing a treaty with Spain that would have Canadianized the fishery over a ten-year period, Spain was a relatively poor country, still suffering the effects of Franco's long dictatorship. It was only when *El Caudillo* died and democracy was restored, by the Constitution of 1976, that Spain began to normalize its commercial relations with other European countries, and these would have been interrupted again if the *coup d'état* mounted by the generals in 1981 had not been put down by King Juan Carlos. Spain entered the E.E.C. only five years later.

In 1981, Spain was in a period of economic restructuring. The Vigo trawler fleet did not yet comprise all the huge, modern fishing units—freezer-trawlers and so on—that it has equipped itself with since. On the contrary, the fleet consisted essentially of large-tonnage ships, but with low technology compared to those of West Germany, Scandinavia, France, Britain, and even Canada. Salting was the rule on the codfishing ships. Many were worn out, having lived a full life, and would have been retired from fishing as the Spanish involvement on the Grand Banks tailed off. In the meantime, the shipowners would have invested in construction of other ships for fishing far from home (the Grand Banks being only 1,500 nautical miles from Vigo), in the Seychelle Islands, along the Namibian coast, or in South America, where hake offered an alternative to cod.

Spain has been a fishing country for centuries; it has long experience and much expertise in harvesting, processing, and marketing ocean products. For the Spanish, fishing is a natural base of development. In 1981, a pivotal year, it would have been easy to plan a strategy for ending fishing on the Grand Banks over a ten-year period. However, not only did

Canada not want to allow Spain this time, but it was becoming more and more arrogant, said many Spaniards, cutting their cod quotas and driving them outside its two-hundred-mile E.E.Z.—alleging a lack of excess resources, although its commissioners were heard chanting the little limerick on the prolific cod stocks in 2J3KL in the Kirby Task Force hearings.

The failure of the agreement had the same effect on Spain as a red cape on a bull, stimulating national pride, combativeness, and not a little bitterness. Since Canada had shown itself reluctant to share even its scientific data on the state of the stocks, Spain decided to profit on its own from the announced abundance of the northern cod.

Since Spain no longer had quotas within the Canadian E.E.Z., where it considered itself to hold historical rights, it would now fish outside the zone. This decision was also based on reasoning of another order. In 1981, after Suarez's centrist government was almost overthrown by the military, there was a strong socialist movement in Spain, one which would in fact bring Felipe Gonzalez to power in 1982. This socialism, not yet the *"descafeinado socialismo"* which Spaniards of a deeper red now scorn, was inspired by the great tradition of humanist and internationalist thought. With regard to fishing philosophy, it agreed with the FAO (the United Nations Food and Agriculture Organization), which, without actually condemning them, questioned the radical changes that had taken place in the conditions of planning and development of fisheries with the extension of coastal nations' jurisdiction to two hundred miles from their shores.

"Ten years ago", Edouard Samoua, director general of the FAO, said in 1982, "most stocks that were not exploited commercially were the property of all. Today, almost all the groundfish stocks, which provide about 90 per cent of world catches, are under the jurisdiction of coastal nations." How would these nations deal with the major responsibility that now fell to them to reconcile optimum use of their resources with the need to respond to the growth in demand for fish for human consumption, which was projected to double, from 55 to 110 million tonnes, between 1980 and 2000? Samoua feared that narrowly nationalistic interests would triumph over the larger concerns of all of humanity.

Fishing the groundfish stocks to the limit of sustainable yield would crown the noble fight against world hunger. Spain therefore had a moral justification for taking from outside the two-hundred-mile zone what Canada was refusing it within the zone.

Portugal's political path was quite similar to that of its neighbour: it freed itself from Salazar and embraced socialism, then social democracy, after the so-called Pink Revolution, when it lost its colonies of Mozambique, Angola, and Guinea. A great fishing nation, considered to hold historical rights to fishing on the Grand Banks and worshipping the *bacalhau* to the point of featuring it at the top of every restaurant menu, Portugal also accepted with poor grace its ejection from the Canadian E.E.Z.

The Canadian fishery has its Achilles heel: the Nose and Tail of the Grand Banks. In the winter, the northern cod migrate to these grounds and the continental slope outside the two-hundred-mile zone, in perfect position for harvesting by the Spanish and Portuguese fleets. In fact, almost all of the northern cod that scatter on the Grand Banks in the summertime are concentrated in these zones in the winter. Although fishing conditions are less favourable in the winter fishery, with its miserable weather, this harvest is controlled only by a loose international organization without any real authority—neither on the high seas nor on paper. After territorial waters were extended to two hundred miles, and two years of vacillation, NAFO (the Northwest Atlantic Fishing Organization) took over administration of the fishery in international waters from ICNAF. Its structure, mandate, and means of action resembled those of its predecessor.

It must be noted, as well, that Canada itself had trouble exercising its authority over its exclusive zone, especially in the winter, not only because of its lack of high-seas coast-guard ships, but because the ice that descends the Davis Strait and the Labrador Sea makes access to the Nose and Tail of the Grand Banks difficult from St. John's.

Reconnaissance flights, which began in 1977, turned up numerous cases of illegal fishing by foreign ships in the Canadian E.E.Z., but these reports were only the tip of the iceberg—bad weather and fog hid the rest. As well, air surveillance, even assisted with high-frequency radar, could not intervene or replace surface patrols. As of 1990, there were only two vessels (one and a half if one counts time in dry dock) to intervene in some 350,000 square miles of ocean. These patrols are therefore, at most, symbolic.

It is all very well to declare one's sovereignty over a territory, but it remains to effectively exercise it. In this, Canada had an obvious weakness: as just one example, when its arctic maritime territory was repeatedly violated by American warships and nuclear submarines, Ottawa raised only anemic protests, when it protested at all, in order not to compromise its "good neighbour" policy.

The Canadian frigates nevertheless sometimes succeeded in finding offenders, boarding and arresting trawlers, and taking them to St. John's for their captains to face Canadian justice. There were also wild chases of Spanish trawlers, sometimes right to the middle of the Atlantic, conflicts which were resolved only by diplomatic intervention. And we must not forget that Canada had analogous and just as serious problems with the Americans at the southern end of its territorial waters: refusals of boarding, chases, even exchanges of fire.

As for the maximum fines of $500,000 for intrusion into the Canadian E.E.Z. and of $750,000 for fishing there—as well as seizure of fishing equipment and fish—if these seemed sufficiently severe and dissuasive on paper, they were much less so in practice, since the penalties imposed by the courts never approached these levels. Thus, the impression was given that Canada considered infractions to the fisheries regulations and the poaching in its E.E.Z. to be mere peccadillos. However, according to the Kirby Report, the catching and processing of a thousand tonnes of fish supplied about twenty person-years of work; the market value of a thousand tonnes of cod before capture was about a million dollars. A trawler illegally fishing sixty tonnes of fish a day was in effect stealing sixty thousand dollars for every day it fishes.

But Canada proved to be annoyingly incapable of tracking down and dealing harshly with marauders. For many foreign captains used to more effective surveillance in their own territorial waters, the Canadian authority was a joke. Under these circumstances, it was inevitable that overfishing of the Nose and the Tail of the Grand Banks in the winter and poaching in the Canadian zone in the summer would intensify as long as "Canadianization" of the cod fishery continued. Whatever guilty afterthoughts this illegal harvest of the resource might have provoked, evaporated under the favourable auspices of an over-evaluation of the northern cod stock by Canadian scientists.

Things went on thus for several years, until the northern cod showed new signs of exhaustion. The reconstruction of the stock that had begun after the E.E.Z. was created, the wellspring of euphoria at the beginning of the 1980s, was over; the charts indicated distressing drops. In the meantime, the two main European fishing nations, Spain and Portugal, had become members of the European Economic Community. This meant that they would no longer be treated as distinct countries in the organization charged with managing the fisheries in the northwest Atlantic, NAFO, but would be part of the European delegation.

When the quotas fixed by NAFO no longer responded to the needs of the EC, in the mid-1980s, the EC made use of an objection procedure included in the organization's constitution that enabled it unilaterally to fix its own quotas. Thus, in 1986, when NAFO imposed a moratorium on cod fishing (quota 0) in zone 2J3KL, even though Canada allowed it takes of 9,500 tonnes by virtue of the Canada-EC Fisheries Agreement, the EC granted itself a unilateral quota of 68,650 tonnes, of which it caught 61,985 tonnes.

Added to Canada's take of northern cod, 266,000 tonnes, a total of about 328,000 tonnes of fish were taken that year from a stock evaluated at just above one million tonnes (biomass of subjects three years and over), of which almost one third, 308,000 tonnes, were reproductively active.

The following year, 1987, having raised its unilateral quota to 76,400 tonnes, while the quota allowed it by NAFO remained at zero—and remains so to this day—the EC caught no more than 35,392 tonnes of northern cod. But this did not keep it from declaring a unilateral quota of 84,000 tonnes for 1988. This could only be interpreted as bravado, since the EC knew very well that the stocks could not tolerate such exploitation. And in fact EC trawlers were able to catch only 26,559 tonnes, one-third of this quota, in that year.

This should have set off alarms. It did so in Canada, which began to reduce its TAC of northern cod, from 266,000 tonnes in 1988 down to 121,000 tonnes by 1992. The latter quota, of course, would never be caught because of the eighteen-month moratorium announced at the beginning of July of that year.

In 1989, the European Community nevertheless assigned itself an initial unilateral quota of 84,000 thousand tonnes of northern cod (Canada having fixed its own quota at 235,000 tonnes), which it agreed to reduce during the year to 58,400 tonnes, and of which it finally caught only 35,594 tonnes. In 1990, a modicum of reason having apparently prevailed, the EC reduced its unilateral quota to 32,000 tonnes, while catches dropped to 21,912 tonnes, in spite of the 130 ships engaged in the fishery.

In any case, in 1991, in spite of a reduction of its unilateral quota to 27,000 tonnes, the EC sent 149 ships to the fishery on the Grand Banks and harvested 23,802 tonnes of northern cod. But the fish were smaller, younger, not having reproduced even once; on top of this, the trawlers had to take a much larger number of individuals in order to obtain the same tonnages.

According to a compilation made from observations by the surveillance flights over the zone controlled by NAFO, the EC fleet was divided as follows: Germany, nine; Portugal, forty-four; Spain, ninety-four; Italy, one; United Kingdom, one. To

these were added ships from nations that were not signatories to the NAFO convention, such as Panama and South
Korea. Since 1986, when they joined the foreign fleet over
NAFOs powerless objections, these marauders have caught
an estimated 165,000 tonnes of fish of all species.

I am sorry to subject the reader to such a flood of numbers,
but it is the only way to give some idea of the extent of the overfishing, unless one wants to measure it (more figures!) in economic terms: if one considers the highest estimates of the value of
the cod before catch, the EC relieved Canada of $205 million
over five years. This figure almost doubles if one takes account
of the catches by ships flying flags of convenience. To these hundreds of millions of dollars must be added, losses due to reductions in Canadian quotas to compensate for the effects of foreign
overfishing, the costs of sustaining the failing economy of the
regions affected by the loss of fish, and now, the half-billion dollars—at least—needed to ride out the eighteen-month moratorium, not to mention the more or less predictable medium- and
long-term after-effects.

This is not simply theft of Canadian property, but a rape of
nature, for which the foreign fleets are responsible: the
squandering of a world nutritional resource, a world-scale environmental catastrophe that can be explained by nothing except the rapaciousness of a civilization that considers
economic progress to be an end in itself. And yet, except in
Canada, where protest is weak as yet, no one is standing up
to denounce it. Nowhere do we see nature lovers marching in
front of embassies brandishing placards and chanting slogans
in defence of the northern cod. Of course, they are very busy
these days, what with the plight of the giant panda, the
elephant, the Florida panther, the Atlantic green turtle, and
so on; they hardly know where to put their hearts, or their
money, which is solicited by a half-dozen "ecological" multi-
national organizations.

Even Canada has remained strangely silent while being
robbed of a resource that was once, along with fur and wood,
its very reason for being. One might have expected that those

who recommended the Canadianization of the fishery and watched as the fish were literally stolen from them, would revolt and raise a ruckus about it. But all of the senators (Leblanc and DeBané, both of whom had held the Fisheries portfolio, and Kirby, now sitting in the upper chamber) do not have the colourful obstinacy of Sen. Jacques Hébert when it comes to standing up for their convictions!

Perhaps the fishery industry should also have raised its voice more loudly. But the companies acted in this matter as they do regarding almost everything that revolve around the fisheries in the Atlantic region: they rely on the government, just as they rely on it for unemployment insurance and for coming up with grants that permit them to make ends meet. With the maritime fisheries industry going from bad to worse over the last twenty years, such reflexes of dependency have become anchored in people's behaviour; they are so imbued with disillusionment and fatalism that fishing communities have lost almost all resiliency or faculty to act independently.

In this regard, one can only meditate on the following comment in the 1990 report by Dr. L. Harris on the state of the northern cod, which I will deal with in the next chapter:

We leave as an open question and one that requires a political answer the issue of whether the fishing should become the preserve of professional fishermen and plant workers, all of whom can earn from it an adequate living; or whether it should continue, as at present, a social relief mechanism, offering some measure of gainful employment and thus of dignity to a large number of participants, most of whom will contine to require income supplementation.

11

Canada's Costly Error

LIKE THE FLOATS OF A NET bobbing in the wake of a trawler, reports and strategy documents mark the course of Canadian fishing policy. Only a few years after the Kirby Task Force announced a "new policy for the Atlantic fisheries," the policy's failure had to be analyzed. Responsibility for this was entrusted by the minister of Fisheries and Oceans, Thomas Siddon, to Dr. Leslie Harris, then rector of Memorial University in St. John's, in 1989. Harris surrounded himself with a team of top-notch scientists, who tackled the rather unpleasant task of conducting a deathbed diagnosis of the moribund northern cod fishery and suggesting ways to resuscitate it.

By the time this "independent" study was ordered, Fisheries and Oceans Canada biologists, along with biometricists and other experts from the Canadian Atlantic Fisheries Scientific Advisory Council (CAFSAC), the agency that fixed the catch quotas for various species each year, had recognized their past errors. They had grossly over-evaluated the recovery of the northern cod stocks after 1977, and had continually fixed the F factor (percentage of exploitable biomass) at an unrealistically high level in the 1980s.

Although the Harris panel acknowledged the weaknesses of its analysis and research tools and the immense complexity of the problem of managing fish, shellfish, mollusk, and sea-mammal stocks that moved over enormous distances and had a wide variety of predatory links with each other (comparing it to "a vast jigsaw puzzle made up of thousands of pieces, each of which is likely to change its shape as we try to make it fit into a picture that also changes as we move along"), it nevertheless was confident that science could determine rational exploitation levels for marine resources.

But it would have to be science without the sin of vanity, which understood that it was itself in a process of self-discovery as it conducted research on its subject, and would not exclude out of hand any information that might contribute to its knowledge. Thus, it considered not only data that it gathered on its own, but also knowledge gained from empirical experience—such as that of the fishermen.

This was the first scientific report that pleaded so vehemently for the inclusion of fishermen in the process of managing marine resources:

> At present, the basic client community, that is to say the fishermen, appear not only to distrust science but fail to understand its nature and its rationale, fail to see the relevance of particular research initiatives to their immediate problems, and fail to appreciate why their vast store of accumulated knowledge based on experience is not taken into account. To address this issue, means must be found to make them feel that they are both stake holders and participants in the process. There is clearly occasion for a community education programme and for the consideration of ways in which the inclusion of fishermen in the planning process can be made more effective.

In fact, the "small" inshore Newfoundland fishermen had since 1986 been predicting the collapse of the northern cod stocks and demanding reductions in the quotas allocated to large industrial trawlers.

Of course, including fishermen in the scientific planning for marine resources is not the cornerstone of the Harris report; nor is its critique of the methodology used by the Fisheries and Oceans Canada scientists, "infected like so many others by the post-1977 euphoria," that led to the collapse of the northern cod stock. The report even conceded that any group of scientists could have committed similar errors under similar circumstances.

Under the influence of this euphoria, the Harris report stated, [the DFO scientists] do not appear to have appreciated the full implications for cod mortality of new technologies and new fishing practices employed by both domestic and foreign fishermen. Confident of their belief that their database and analytical methods were sound and, hence, that the F0.1 management strategy was indeed a functional reality they were prepared to accept the results of their assessment techniques and to set aside as aberrational certain signs that might have been interpreted as pointing in another direction. Without benefit of hindsight, they were predisposed to accept even when optional data interpretations were possible, those tending to support the validity of their mathematical models.

In fairness, of course, we must recognize that fisheries population dynamics is by nature a complex matter influenced by a wide variability in environmental, behavioural, and general ecological elements that constitute the ecological system. . . . In the view of the Panel, the methods used by DFO scientists to make the pieces fit were not notably faulty in concept but were based on tenuous conclusions and skimpy data sets.

In other words, the Fisheries and Oceans scientists were being reproached for relying too much on certain trawls conducted from their research vessel, which indicated a heartening abundance of northern cod, and for having favoured these data to "tune" (as I explained in a previous chapter) their virtual-population, or cohort, analyses made from fishing data by age class—that is, the figures from the trawlers' catch reports. Given the relatively small number of soundings by the research vessels, a wide variety of factors or combinations of factors, even those that had been measured (water temperature, plankton content, winds, currents, migratory paths, date, location, etc.), can affect the data in unforeseen ways. In short, the Harris panel concluded, five or six weeks per year of sampling stocks on board a research vessel was insufficient to gather the data needed to determine the catch levels for all commercial species on the east coast of Canada. The best laboratories and the most sophisticated software would never replace the collection of data on the high seas, and the scientists simply didn't spend enough time there.

It was a question of budgets, protested Fisheries and Oceans. Irrelevant, replied the Harris report: if the government cannot afford a research vessel for more than five or six weeks a year, agreements should be made with owners for the scientists to be sent out on commercial ships. This would have the added benefit of putting researchers in contact with fishermen.

This was the first error committed by the biometricists. The second consisted of over-evaluating, year after year, the F factor, which determined the level at which a stock could be fished. Even if there were gaps in the data or errors in the evaluation methods for fish populations, fishing quotas still had to be established. "The world will simply not stand still," the Harris panel stated, "while we await more perfect knowledge."

> But [the report continued], knowing that our science is, in consequence, found to be inexact, we must be all the more careful in using the tools we do possess and the knowledge we do command to the best advantage and always with a determination to err, if err we must, on the side of prudent caution. Even though we have suggested elsewhere that the miscalculations of DFO scientists in respect of the growth of the northern cod stock up to 1988 might have been committed by any other scientific group given similar circumstances, we might also suggest that the problem might have been sooner identified had there been a greater appreciation of the weakness of our science and a greater commitment to caution.
>
> . . .
>
> The management strategy adopted in 1977 was that designated as $F_{0.1}$ which would have meant fishing at an instantaneous mortality rate of about 0.18. Instead fishing mortality was maintained at a level of at least $F_{0.4}$, and possibly higher.

This means that the northern cod were being fished much more quickly than they could reproduce. It is possible that, in some years, quotas permitted fishing of northern cod at the shocking rate of $F_{0.62}$—that is, that 62 per cent of its total biomass was being taken!

It is hardly surprising that, under these circumstances, the EC granted itself such high quotas. Using approximately the same biometric techniques as the Canadians, notwithstanding errors in evaluation, the European scientists concluded- that Canada was wildly exploiting its cod stocks. On the other hand, they heard Canadian representatives preaching virtue at ICNAF meetings, asking foreign fleets to cut back their catch, recommending—and finally obtaining—a moratorium on fishing "their" northern cod in international waters, although their own trawlers were authorized to deplete the stocks within the two-hundred-mile limit.

It is easy to imagine that the Europeans would see this contradiction as very suspicious, and would interpret the Canadian recommendations to ICNAF as a move in a sordid game of "bluff". In this context, they would have said to themselves, "If Canada wants to clean out its northern cod stocks for its profit alone, we won't stand there with our hands tied; we'll help them, by God, and very efficiently, to boot!"

Of course, sincerity, good faith, and honesty are so deeply woven into the Canadian social fabric, including Québec, that its citizens are often seen as guileless, or even disarmingly naïve, in the eyes of other countries with a more naturally wily spirit. But where the northern cod were concerned, the European fishing nations were forced to question their first impression: perhaps this was just a façade, hiding an infinitely more cunning personality. To signal that they were not fooled by the Canadian strategy, the Europeans raised their unilateral quota from 76,000 tonnes in 1987 to 84,000 tonnes in 1988. Were not the Canadians, bitterly complaining of shortages, also raising their own quota from 256,000 to 266,000 tonnes?

Paradoxically, there is, in fact, a kind of absurd logic to overfishing, which postulates enabling the fish stocks to recover, albeit only over the very long term. The Harris report suggested that the federal government seriously consider resorting to this unusual reasoning in the context of foreign overfishing on the Nose and Tail of the Grand Banks. Simply put, Canadian trawlers would be sent to participate in the rape of the northern cod alongside the foreign ships.

The logic went like this: since foreign trawlers were taking all of the available fish, participation of Canadian trawlers would not affect the total cod take, and therefore would not damage the stock any further, but instead would distribute the catch over a larger number of ships so that fishing would be less profitable for everyone, notably the foreigners. Eventually, it would no longer be economically feasible for anyone to continue, and everyone would be forced to abandon the fishery, finally giving some respite to the resource so that it could recover. In the meantime, Canada's negotiators could use the situation to demonstrate to its NAFO partners the obvious need to endow the agency with teeth to enforce the regulations, in the best interest of all parties.

It is understandable, though hardly commendable, that the Europeans would use the same reasoning as they saw Canada continuing to overfish in 1987, 1988, and 1989. Since they were in no way claiming a monopoly on virtue at the NAFO table, they did not hesitate to give chase...

It must be remembered that the Harris panel's *Independent Review of the State of the Northern Cod* did not hold foreign overfishing on the Nose and Tail of the Grand Banks solely responsible for the shocking decline of the northern cod, the fish stock most important to the Canadian fisheries, providing (at any rate, before the moratorium) 40 per cent of the cod landed on the east coast of Canada. Although the report did not minimize the disastrous impact of the foreign fleets, it also examined other factors that have contributed, and still contribute, to the decline of the cod. They cannot be listed in order of importance, since none is precisely calculable, but all have an appreciable impact, according to the Harris panel, on the abundance of the cod, and the fishermen often talk about them: seals, ghost nets, bycatches, discards, water salinity, and so on. Very fortunately, the remarkable scientists on the panel, L. Harris, D.L. Alverson, John G. Pope, Robert D. Fournier, Maxfield Short, Frank D. Smith, and Mary Lou Peters, listened attentively to what these fishermen had to say.

12

Fish to Drown

AS I MENTIONED ABOVE, other factors besides fishing can influence the abundance or paucity of northern cod (or any other stock), although they are not calculated, or even calculable, nor can they be ranked in order of importance. It is not even certain that we know what they all are.

First, there are bycatches, or what is caught aside from the species that is intentionally being fished. There are regulations that aim to limit these, for obvious conservation reasons. A trawler cannot have in its hold more than a certain percentage (10 per cent, as a general rule) of a species other than the one it is licensed to fish.

When this threshold is reached, bycatches pose a thorny problem of conscience to the trawler captain. He can either break the law and keep the fish—without noting them in his catch report—risking a stiff fine if his ship is thoroughly inspected, or throw them back into the sea, and generally underevaluate their quantity in his report. It is always distressing for a fisherman to throw the fruit of his labour back into the sea; on the other hand, he fears that if the authorities knew the exact size of his discards, they would limit his access to other species. In any case, the fish loses, for it is dead, and the statistics are skewed.

If one multiplies the unreported cod bycatches by the hundred trawlers with a license to fish other species in Canada's E.E.Z., one begins to see how significantly this phenomenon affects the total biomass of cod, as well as its calculation by the scientists.

These discards are particularly disastrous when they consist of small, immature fish, like the tiny one-year-old cod that live in the benthic depths and are often found among shrimp catches. It is estimated that in certain seasons, as many of these small fish are discarded as shrimp are kept on board. Here again, afraid of having their permits restricted to less favourable seasons or zones, fishing captains have a tendency to greatly underreport the discards.

Under some circumstances, the amount of fish discarded to meet the legal percentage of bycatches can practically caricature the ridiculousness of some of the regulations designed to protect the resource. A fisherman friend of mine who had just returned from a trip to catch redfish off the west coast of Newfoundland in the autumn of 1991 told me that at this particular time of that year, the redfish in St. Georges Bay, sheltered by the high counterforts of the Anguille Mountains, were mixed in almost equal parts with cod—and not cod that were too small to fillet, but good-sized fish. After the first trawl, his quota of cod bycatch had been reached; after that, to finish filling his hold, he had to discard as many good cod as he kept redfish. My friend still had a heavy heart as he told me this story, not because of the great money he would have earned, but because of the sheer waste.

A simple calculation shows the horrible folly of the bycatch regulations: in this case, to fish two hundred and some tonnes of redfish (one load for a trawler of this class), almost two hundred tonnes of cod had to be discarded. Well, one might say, actually, this fish has been lost only to humans; once thrown back, even dead, even decomposing into mineral salts if not devoured by a predator, it has still been recycled into the great biological soup of the ocean.

Maybe. But the trawler on which my friend was working was one among twenty, all trawling the same fishing grounds and complaining to each other over the ship radio about having thrown similar quantities of cod back into the sea. Even accounting for exaggeration, always a factor in fishing stories, it is obvious that a significant percentage of the TAC of Gulf cod (40,000 tonnes in that zone) was lost without a trace on this occasion.

A significant percentage is also wasted even when cod *is* the actual target, each time a captain casts his trawl for a final tow to fill one last compartment of the hold that can still take four or five tonnes of fish. He might harvest, depending on the size of his gear and the trawling time, twenty tonnes or more of cod. What doesn't fit into the hold is tossed overboard—and, obviously, not included in the catch report, resulting in yet another falsification in the biometric estimates.

The impact on the stocks of this practice varies directly with the catching power of the ship, and its frequency is generally much higher than thought. The fisheries management bureaucrats who qualify it as "marginal" must be out of touch with the realities of work on a trawler deck! Of course, no sign of it is found in the catch reports, and the fishermen don't breathe a word. It is one of the secrets of the sea, one of those things one doesn't mention when one returns to land, like the location of a fishing bank, the escapades in bawdy houses at ports away, the hookers at fifty dollars a pop, and all the rest.

Even research vessels are not immune to this waste. At each tow of their trawl (averaging between 1,000 and 1,500 kg of fish), they only keep 500 individuals for the biologists' work. The rest, up to ten tonnes a day, is discarded, as a biologist shocked by the practice told me.

"What can we do about it?" I can hear the civil servants moan, throwing their hands in the air. "After all, we can't have an inspector on board every fishing vessel!"

True—although if one considers the price of a tonne of cod before it is caught, it would perhaps be a wise investment. But there are less expensive surveillance methods. For instance, an instrument could be used that is found in more and more households, that is not very bothersome, and that has an ever lower price tag (a trifle compared with the treasure trove of electronic equipment found in the wheelhouses of large trawlers): a video camera. If there were one on every trawler, a sort of equivalent to the black boxes found on airplanes, with a wide-angle view of the fishing deck, and triggered by the mechanisms that raise and lower the trawl, it would automatically provide a visual record of the catch, along with valuable information on its size and composition (percentage of cod, redfish, ray, plaice, etc.). If it could be linked to the LORAN, information on the longitude and latitude of each trawling run would also be available. What didn't appear on screen, hidden by a fisherman's boot or by the tackle, could then truly be considered a negligible quantity.

However, this still would not eliminate the folly of the bycatch regulations that require perfectly good fish to be thrown back into the sea. Ideally, there should be no discards at all, and especially not of species for which there is a market, in Canada or elsewhere. Under such a system, the capacity of the hold would limit the total biomass caught. This would force the industry, among other things, to find ways to market unpopular species. With a few exceptions, other countries do manage to market them; given the globalization of economic activity, there is no reason for the Canadian fisheries industry not to do more in this respect.

One objection to this scheme is that fishermen will intentionally fish the most profitable species and pass them off as bycatch. Of course, the new rules must also have teeth—shark's teeth, if necessary. Levels of abuse and recidivism could be determined and violations punished by fines or even by cancellation of permits, pure and simple. As for reasonable cases in which an allocated species other than the one intentionally fished has been caught above its permissible bycatch limit, the quantity fished in excess of the quota for the species could be deducted from the ship's quota (when one exists) or from the company's, or from both, or could be divided with the region, the province, or the country: the important thing would be to use this biomass in the best possible way and to deduct it from the official catch quota for the stock, since it has in fact been caught.

A less simple and infinitely nastier problem is the presence of ghost nets. These are gillnets made of nylon or other non-biodegradable synthetic fibres (unlike their predecessors, which were made of plant fibres); lost by fishermen during storms, they continue to fish, adrift, catching their quarry by the gills. The fish die, rot, and decompose, leaving the net free to trap other unfortunate individuals. Unless a storm or other violent perturbation of the ocean rolls them into a ball or shreds them, ghost nets can continue to fish for many years.

The problem is not a new one. I first heard it raised by fishermen from Québec's North Shore at the Gaspé Fisheries Economic Summit in 1978. At the time, fishermen from Harrington Harbour to Blanc Sablon were complaining about the Newfoundland government's assistance programme that replaced lost gillnets for free. All the fishermen had to do was report their loss to a provincial fisheries department office, and they were given a new net. The result was that they didn't spend much time looking for their lost nets: the ocean is deep, the horizon wide, and time precious for everyone.

No one knows exactly how many gillnets were lost over the time this programme lasted, but some speculate that there were several thousand, perhaps tens of thousands. With nets several hundred fathoms long, there is mesh aplenty to keep inflicting a completely useless mortality on the fish. Assuming that some of them are solidly snagged on rocks, seaweed, or deepsea cliffs, there is no reason for them not to still be working twenty, or even fifty, years from now.

One thing is certain: the problem is real. Many fishermen have found nets full of decomposing fish in their trawls. And another thing is certain: the problem persists, although no doubt on a diminishing scale since Newfoundland has stopped supporting free replacement of these nets. There are always fishermen using gilllnets, and there are always storms that wash them away so that they can't be found, even if they are looked for.

Their are differences of opinion as to the amount of damage they cause, depending on whether one asks a fisherman who uses gillnets, long lines, traps, or a trawl. The issue puts into play the rivalries not just between inshore and off-shore fishermen, but also between fishermen with different types of fixed gear, each of whom considers his tackle to be the best for both the catch and the resource. In any case, ghost nets are sufficiently destructive that they are a subject of concern on the coast—and discussed in the Harris report.

Most disturbing of all is that unless the entire sea bed is raked, we will not get rid of them.

Another issue that has a direct impact on the cod stocks, according to many fishermen and the Harris report, could be eliminated, or at least contained, but this will not be done for fear of an international outcry. It is the Greenland seal (*Pagophilus groenlandicus*—"Greenland lover of ice").

After the seal hunt was banned, in 1983, following a boycott of seal products by the EC, the Canadian Department of Fisheries and Oceans simply stopped counting seals for many years. Only in 1991 was the herd evaluated, but without using the sophisticated methods (aerial ultraviolet location, gridding of the ice floes, etc.) that had been employed when the goal was to ensure the seals' defenders that their protégés were faring well in spite of the hunt.

However, whether the Greenland seals are being hunted or not, it is essential to have a fairly accurate idea of their numbers because they are voracious predators, each individual consuming between one and one-and-a-half tonnes per year, and are situated at the top of the food chain. Whether there are between two and two-and-a-half million of them, as was the case when the hunt stopped, or four to six million, as is estimated today, they certainly have an impact on the marine ecosystem. Even if their number and their appetite are es-timated at a minimum, they are still greater consumers of fishery resources than all of the fishing fleets, Canadian and foreign, in the northwest Atlantic!

But we don't know how many Greenland seals there are in the herd, and when one remarks to fisheries managers that it might be important to know this in order to gauge their impact on the cod, the response is a shrug of the shoulders and an *ex cathedra* pronouncement: "Greenland seals don't eat cod." Not only is this untrue (the International Fund for Animal Welfare, the main adversary of the seal hunt, placed an ad in all the newspapers with a picture showing fifty baby seals of which at least one—2 per cent of those shown—was in fact clearly eating cod), but it does not prevent the seals from being major consumers of capelin (their most important source of protein), which is a favourite staple of the cod. This alone reveals a correlation between the two species.

Seals also eat certain benthic shrimp, as well as mollusks and small fish that cod feed on. In fact, all small animals that seals consume can also be part of the cod diet, since the cod eat everything—including, in times of food shortage, stones, to digest the algae that grow on them.

Seals do not turn up their noses at cod when they're available. Canadian research has shown that cod was found in 2 per cent of the stomachs of seals caught on the ice floes by coastal seal hunters—about the same percentage as in the IFAW ad. Nothing terribly controversial there! However, this research was conducted at a time in the seal's biological cycle (whelping, mating, moulting) when it is reputed to fast, and the individuals studied had all been caught near the coast, where there is very little cod at that time of year. What happens when the seals meet the compact (as much as they can still be) schools of cod in the high seas at the end of their fast, remains to be studied.

Fishermen from the Magdalen Islands, who asked Fisheries and Oceans Canada for a small grant to go out in ships with biologists (they were interested in determining the quantity of snow crab devoured by the seals), found out that research on this aspect of seals was not a very high priority. Their request was turned down. Yet government scientists keep claiming that there is no proof seals have a significant impact on the cod (or crab) stocks, and they refute the observations of fishermen tending to demonstrate the opposite on the pretext that they are not "scientific". The fishermen face skepticism similar to that of a certain recent U.S. president, who would have had to see the marble columns adorning the façade of the White House disintegrating before his very eyes before he would concede that an acid-rain problem existed.

Fast forward. In Newfoundland, last spring, the captain of the *Northern Storm*, the largest fishing trawler on the east coast of Canada, purchased in the Faroe Islands, gave me another image: when he lifted his net the previous fall, in the Labrador Sea, there were as many seals around, trying to snatch the fish from the nets, as there were gulls overhead. Anyone who has seen the clouds of hungry gulls wheeling above a trawler when the net is winched up, literally filling the air with their piercing cries, would have a good idea of just how many seals there were.

During public hearings held by the Harris panel in Newfoundland coastal villages, many fishermen mentioned predation of the cod by seals. Small semi-offshore trawler crews reported that the stomachs of seals caught in their nets were full of cod and turbot, while the inshore fishermen observed an increased frequency of cod with devoured stomachs in their nets. Apparently, the seals have a marked preference for cod stomachs, while the flesh of the fish seems to be much less palatable to them. This is corroborated by seal hunters from the Newfoundland Front, who have seen eviscerated cod on the ice near where they found seals, which can be explained by the fact that cod are predators of capelin, itself a favourite food of the Greenland seal.

Similar observations were made by researchers from the University of Tromsø in northern Norway. There too, cod fishermen were persuaded that Greenland seals were providing them with stiff competition, so the Norwegian biologists went to see for themselves. They surrounded with nets a wide expanse of sea in which there were various species of fish and seals, and then went diving.

They observed that Greenland seals chased almost any fish they encountered, and sometimes took only one bite before veering off toward another prey that looked more appetizing. They thus destroyed many more fish than they consumed, notably cod, which were not among their favourites when there were other species around. They attacked the cod anyway, and killed them before abandoning them for a choicer morsel. They were not only voracious, but sloppy, eaters.

Of course, science cannot observe, list, and quantify exactly what happens when several million seals, hungry after their long, nonstop migration from the Arctic, meet the capelin-gorged cod in the region of the banks of Labrador and Newfoundland toward the end of the autumn. But denying that seals prey on cod under the pretext that there is no scientific proof shows an annoying, selective blindness to the natural order of things.

The minimum that we should expect from the managers of our marine resources is that they, like Harris, recognize the necessity of considering "the question of how long a [fishing] system predicated upon an annual and controlled harvest of commercially valuable marine species can remain viable if all the major components of the system but one are subject to TACs, and that one is subject to no control at all." In other words, seals should be submitted at least to a serious census.

Should the seals be hunted again to cull a considerable number as quickly as possible, as almost all fishermen hope? It is easy to envision the passionate worldwide debate that the issue will undoubtedly engender. (Crocodile) tears will no doubt be spilled again by some tender-hearted urban ecologists, who forget that our wild and beautiful nature is also savage and cruel, and who, ironically, are the greatest despoilers of it because of their very life style. Not only are many infected, to various degrees, with the disease of over-consumption, but their detritus, pollution and trash, inevitably ends up in the ocean, altering its capacity to produce life. Black tides are the direct result of such an energy-hungry life-style. As well, discarded nitric compounds such as fertilizer run-off favour the growth of algae which consume oxygen and literally choke the ocean and the fish in it. These infestations, or "blooms", have been reported all over the planet in the last ten years.

As well, pollution has a pernicious effect on plankton production. This is actually the cornerstone of the issue, since to produce a kilo of animal plankton (zooplankton) requires ten kilos of plant plankton (phytoplankton, produced by the photosynthesis of nitrates and phosphates resulting from the decomposition of dead organisms). In the same way, filtering organisms and small predators must consume roughly a kilo of zooplankton to obtain a weight gain of 100 grams; the ratio is again ten to one, when these organisms are consumed by little fish, since these fish transform about 90 per cent of their food into energy, sometimes a bit more, sometimes a bit less, depending on their way of life.

The same ratio applies when the cod consume these small fish—capelin, herring, mackerel, and so on. In fact, it has been established that an adult cod corresponds to thirty tonnes of phytoplankton; a fifty-kilo tuna, an extremely active fish, to five thousand tonnes. These figures are breathtaking when multiplied by the total biomass of the fishing resources, and stupefying given the formidable biological productivity of the oceans. And they are all the more frightening when one considers that the tiniest variation in plankton production at the bottom of the food chain can have huge repercussions up the line.

There is no question that the system is very, very sick. The total biomass of northwest Atlantic fish stocks in 1990 was, at most, half of the 2.3 million tonnes (all species together) that it was in 1970, after the overfishing of the 1960s. Moreover, some commercial species might never recover, their ecological niche being taken up by other, hardier, more agressive species. The surge of the dogfish (a small shark) while cod was in decline could be an indicator of this phenomenon.

13

Meanwhile, in Newfoundland

St. John's, 29 March 1992

IT WAS BY PURE ACCIDENT that I found myself in the crowd gathered on the dock to hear speeches and homilies before a trawler fleet cast off for the high seas to make a symbolic protest against foreign overfishing beyond the two-hundred-mile limit. But it was no accident that this was the date chosen by the Newfoundland Fishermen, Food and Allied Workers Union (NFFAWU) to organize its demonstration against foreign overfishing. Forty-three years earlier, on this date, Newfoundland had become the tenth province (some would say, prisoner) of Canada.

There was much ill feeling and resentment in the crowd, especially among the older people, listening to the parade of speakers and preachers onstage. The voices, broadcast over a powerful P.A. system, echoed and became distorted as they bounced off the side of a multi-storey public parking building, full of people, and the walls of old warehouses. The St. John's harbour likely had not seen such hordes of people since the legendary times of the sealing ships at the beginning of the century.

After exhortations to the political powers in Ottawa proffered by union leaders and local politicians, the ministers of various churches, perhaps more realistic, addressed their pleas to the All-Powerful, then proposed a prayer. In the silence, I saw heads bowed, revealing the powerful necks of ocean workers with skin weathered by the sun, the salt, and the wind.

"O Lord Almighty, bless Thee this dragger fleet..."

Next came the singing of "O Canada". From the huge crowd only a few weak voices were raised, so that the anthem was hardly louder than the prayer. Calixa Lavallée's hymn has doubtlessly been rendered with more fervour! As the last bars faded, with sparsely scattered and thin voices loudly shrieking "We stand on guard for thee" as if to make up for the silence of others, "Ode to Newfoundland" was announced. Now, heads rose and from every throat the melody and words poured out. From the docks full of people rose a powerful, proud clamour that buried the voice of the person singing at the microphone, rolling along the slopes of the old fjord that forms the harbour, spreading beyond the Battery and the Narrows to mix with the sharp cries of the gulls and the murmuring of the waves.

Ted Anderson, from Makkovik, who was with me, threw out his chest and seemed to be almost warm, although he was dressed just in a jacket and tie.

Earlier, Ted had told me that he wasn't of legal age to vote when Joe Smallwood called the referendums for joining Canada, but he would have voted for it wholeheartedly. If the same choice were before him today, he would vote no. "They took everything from us," he said. "We had our seal hunt, but it's gone. And now the cod is gone too."

This is the litany of the many Labradorians and Newfoundlanders who are still as bound up in the traditional ways of life as they are to the Rock, where they built their homes beside the ocean. The Ottawa bureaucrats have banned the seal hunt because the Europeans didn't want the seals killed any more, let the Europeans pillage the cod, and gave them Labrador's backcountry forest as a training area for NATO low-altitude fighter jets. There was no love lost in Newfoundland and Labrador for the federal government in this respect.

The most cruel of Newfoundland jokes being circulated these days goes something like this. The decisive factor in favour of the "yes" vote in the second referendum on Newfoundland joining Canada (carried by a whisker) was the vaunted social coverage the new country offered: the panacea of unemployment insurance. In this regard, Confederation has been a success beyond Newfoundlanders' wildest dreams: while Canada lured them with the bright promise of the Hibernia oil fields, it quietly took away the seal hunt, let

Québec swindle them out of the electricity from the Churchill Falls at rock-bottom prices, and allowed their fish stocks to be destroyed. Then, when the seals and cod, the pillars of life, were gone, Canada was to let Hibernia slip away too, although the project might be re-activated, so that now the Rock would have only full-timeunemployment insurance for sustenance. Thus was the main promise of union with Canada fulfilled beyond all expectations!

When the negotiators of the latest round of constitutional discussions talked about devolving the financing and management of unemployment insurance to the provinces, Newfoundlanders smiled grimly. Now, after spoiling everything, Ottawa wanted to kick them back out of its blessed program. What did they take them for, a bunch of Newfies?

All of this ran through my mind as "Ode to Newfoundland" ended on strong notes that expressed the attachment, the fervour, the love of people for this rough-hewn Rock battered by the waves, and the hope that one day it might live up to the dream that was still alive in people's memories. Then people looked at each other, a little surprised that they had all sung with such heartfelt vigour. The fog seemed less leaden, the wind a little gentler. Spring was but eight days old; there was still quite a bit of time until next winter. All of their faith was placed in these seven trawlers draped with flags and placards, their railings still full of passengers, reporters, and cameras, which would soon cast off with a great racket of wailing sirens that would reach the pit of their stomachs, to go and tell the Spanish and Portuguese that this nonsensical pillage must stop.

Later, everyone gathered on the heights of the Battery, like a scene from a David Blackwood etching, to watch the fleet reach the Narrows, round the cape, and head for the far reaches of the ocean from which they had all come.

It was by accident, pure and simple, that I was there. A group of Newfoundland environmentalists had been searching for a Québec counterpart who would join with them to confirm the indisputable Canadian-ness of a new pressure group that was being formed to dramatize the cod shortage. Not knowing anyone, they had contacted a Montreal communications firm, which flipped through its Rolodex and gave them my phone number, although I don't belong to any environmental organization.

I then received a phone call from the head of this newborn organization, Stan Tobin, who convinced me at least to go to Newfoundland for a preliminary meeting, attend the demonstration, of course, and meet with foreign journalists invited by the federal Department of External Affairs in an attempt to raise awareness in Europe of the need for their fleets to stop overfishing on the Nose and Tail of the Grand Banks. All of this fell within the diplomatic approach favoured by Canada to solve the dispute; the organizers of this media offensive felt that, along with fishermen's committees, union leaders, company owners, managers, bureaucrats, and scientists—biometricists and others—the "environmentalists" would nicely round out the group.

Although this was terribly last-minute, and I had to put off some work I had planned, I was happy when I landed in St. John's. After I checked in at the hotel, I took a walk down the streets I knew well—Water, Duckworth—and the narrow stairway alleys that link them. I've always liked St. John's, with its large wooden houses painted in deep, dark colours tucked into the slopes of the fjord, its steep streets, its small, dishevelled squares adorned with a few trees that pop up without warning at intersections, and the horizon that widens as one climbs the hills. As well as being the oldest city in North America, it is one of the most beautiful.

At least, it was. Modernization has, in St. John's as elsewhere, led to a mushrooming of characterless glass-and-concrete cubes which are usually ill-matched to the old wooden houses. Empty lots awaiting new construction punch holes in the façades, and the ever-growing number of parking lots oppress the spirit of the old buildings.

On this first evening, it was late, it was cold, and I couldn't find in the pubs the lively seaport ambience they once had. St. John's, like all Canadian Atlantic ports, was then closed to foreign fishing vessels except in emergencies: this was one of Canada's retaliatory measures for their pillage of the cod. But it had taken away lots of business, some grumbled, from the ship-chandlers, the shipyards, and the taverns. Saint-Pierre had inherited this trade.

"For all it does," the proprietor of a fish-and-chips restaurant in which I was the last, late customer, told me, "we could let them back in. Then at least we would get something from it!" (They are now permitted back in, as a result of an "historical" agreement between the E.C. and Canada on fishing 2J3KL cod.) On the wall was a poster, a little dog-eared, which used to be ubiquitous in Newfoundland. Above a huge picture of the venerated fish was the inscription "In Cod We Trust", to which a realist had added, in parentheses, the letters "ED", relegating this faith to the past.

"It's terrible, terrible and disastrous!" exclaimed Moya Cahill, a young, distinguished naval engineer and a member of our group of environmentalists, in the office of her thriving company overlooking the port, the next day. "Once, when friends visited from the mainland, we took my father's boat and went out just beyond the Narrows, where we caught tuna. Tuna! Imagine...to catch cod, all we had to do was drop the jigger into the water and bring it up, and one was hooked. They were all over the place. Last summer, I took friends out in the boat and we jigged the entire afternoon without catching a single fish."

Ted Anderson told us about the three lonely cod caught at Makkovik the previous year, adding that there had been traps and ships full of cod two months of the year just twenty years before. Cod that had gotten smaller over the years, proof that they were disappearing.

In a long, smoky conference room, Ted Anderson also told foreign journalists, pointing to his face, that if there were no fur on the edge of his parka hood, his face would freeze in the terrible winter cold "up north". Hunting seals and trapping were vital activities, like fishing. Obviously, it was his way of life that the Europeans were destroying with their decimation of the cod stock, although he also knew that they weren't the only ones to overfish.

"I tell you, my friends," he concluded, "if we don't deal with these problems before the day is over, there will be more serious ones tomorrow. For all of us. For you too."

Ted was calm and intense, looking young for his sixty-something years, proud of his Innu blood, and obviously ill at ease and awkward in a sport jacket and tie. He hadn't been to St. John's in seven years.

Paul Linegar was much more comfortable in his blue blazer and grey-flannel trousers, polished shoes, white shirt, and striped tie, although he was perfectly aware that he too was wearing a costume—or, rather, his work clothes. He is a lawyer and a naturalist, a biologist armed with the sword of Themis.

Linegar has lively, spirited eyes behind little glasses: he listens first and speaks later. For him last March, it was imperative that Canada immediately exercise the powers it had according the Law of the Sea and manage unilaterally its cod population on the border of the E.E.Z., since it had proved impossible to come to satisfactory agreements with other countries, notably the European Community. The text of the law is clear with regard to "straddling stocks", which migrate between two jurisdictions, or are "seated between two chairs".

But it is one thing to declare one's intention to enforce the law, and another thing actually to do so. Since all of the overfishing was taking place in international waters, Canada could go so far as to send out navy ships, firing warning shots, if necessary. Instead, it opted for the diplomatic route.

Earlier in March, Linegar told me, the fishermen's union had invited to Newfoundland some comrades from Iceland, to learn how they had managed to drive the British trawlers outside of their fishing zone in what made headlines around the world as the "Cod War." The Icelanders had brought the answer with them: huge, long-sleeved jemmies. With this weapon, they went up to the English trawlers and, snap! to starboard, snap! to port, they cut the trawling cables. As simple as that! Unrecoverable, on the bottom, lay the *corpus delictus*. The whole outfit, including net, doors, ropes, bobbins, floats, cables, and labour, could be worth up to $100,000. It gave the English pause.

There had been two cod wars: the first to force foreigners back to twenty-five miles from the Iceland coast, the second to fifty miles. There was no need to do more: the cod migrate no farther in the winter. Some Newfoundlanders were eager to emulate the blond Vikings of Reykjavik. However, the Icelandic fishermen who had cut the cables were backed up by small coast-guard gunships in their sabotage missions, ready to intervene if need be. Canada refused to support such piracy on the high seas by the Newfoundlanders; diplomacy was the rule.

One strategy remained, which Canada resisted, but this time in the name of virtue: let the Newfoundland trawlers participate in the rape of the cod on the Nose and Tail of the Grand Banks with the foreign fleets. Linegar, like Harris, felt that this strategy had been abandoned too quickly and should be reconsidered. More trawlers at work, as I have explained, would not mean that significantly more cod would be taken, since they were already being fished to the maximum by more than a hundred trawlers. However, the catch of each ship would be reduced, and that was the point: the profits would also be divided. Perhaps the fleets from Vigo and Porto would then find it less advantageous to cross the Atlantic.

Linegar's eyes glinted maliciously, then he quickly smiled. He knew that Canada wanted to be a paradigm of virtue at the NAFO table. Otherwise, how could its word be trusted?

That evening, no one could pry open a hole for our group in the very full schedule of a new delegation of journalists, so Stan Tobin, president and soul of the Newfoundland and Labrador Environmental Association, invited me to his home in Ship Cove, on Placentia Bay. As we drove through Argentia, the old capital (1622–92), when Newfoundland belonged to France, he pointed out fishing ships moored in double and triple rows at the docks, vessels that would have been at sea in this season, in normal years. Hovering around the processing plants and the other port installations was a strange atmosphere of idleness, discouragement, uncertainty: the ghosts of dreary tomorrows.

Of the six houses in Ship Cove, only Stan's is still inhabited; the failure of the fishery has driven out the other residents. But he didn't want to leave, even though he had seen the same failure as the others. When the cod began to decline, he had switched to fishing lumpfish, the roe of which is highly appreciated by gourmets. This worked well at the beginning, but then the government multiplied the fishing permits, as it always does, striking the fatal blow: overproduction, a drop in prices, and depletion of the stocks followed. Stan sold his tackle, but the stubborn Irishman in him would not admit defeat.

With his wife, Dolores, he turned to raising sheep and Highland cattle, which graze freely in the countryside. One of the abandoned houses (he bought them all for a song) became a small butter factory, producing the "ship butter" that the Grand Banks schooners once bought from people in the outports. The blocks, formed in old wood moulds retrieved from attics, are purchased all over Newfoundland. To help make ends meet, Stan also was a consultant on various environmental committees. He could thus continue to live where he was born, in the magnificent, wild country of rock and spruce, face to the ocean and back to the immense forest, from which a caribou or an elk sometimes emerged to graze in his front yard.

But, so far from everything—his closest neighbour is fifteen kilometres away—with the incessant siren calls of the city on the airwaves, with the videos and music, the fantasies of Eros and abundance touted everywhere by advertising, would Stan's three sons follow in his wake—or his furrow, actually, now that he had had to abandon the fishery and work the land? Is it possible to resuscitate outports whose very existence was based on the cod that are no more? His two elder sons, who took me back to St. John's, admitted that they didn't know. They loved the solitude and tranquillity of Ship Cove. It was their home. But there were no jobs, no social life to speak of. It was a one-family village. First they would go to university, then they would see.

14

Looking for a Media Bomb

THE EUROPEAN JOURNALISTS invited to St. John's were, with a couple of exceptions, masters of skepticism, among the least gullible in the trade. The Spaniard, employed by a fisheries-industry journal in Vigo, and the Portuguese reporter both denied that there was overfishing or that the cod stocks were truly in peril. The French educational-television team wanted to hear nothing about the carnage the seals were wreaking on the cod. The Icelander sarcastically remarked that his country had not managed to impede over-fishing even though it was now the exclusive manager of its marine resources, and he strongly doubted that Canada would beat the odds: the trawlers were too destructive, the need to make the investments profitable too overwhelming. The Briton, very Oxonian with wispy blond hair falling in his eyes and his polka-dot tie on his checked shirt, protested that his country wasn't participating in the rape, and the German took refuge in his good conscience, for his country had only a single trawler, which surely must have come from the ex-GDR.

The Norwegian journalist was sympathetic: the fishermen of her country were also suffering from a ban on hunting seals—and whales—while the fish that they were still allowed to catch were getting ever scarcer. They had actually scuttled some vessels to reduce their catching power. In most fishing ports, there was recession, even crisis, just as there was in Newfoundland. Perhaps the future of the sea lay in with fish farming, at which the Norwegians excel.

One can, of course, think of it this way: fishermen are anachronistic hunter-gatherers finally undergoing their neolithic revolution.

The distressing predicament of the Newfoundland cod did not, in the end, make headlines or move the masses in

Europe. It produced only small ripples and wavelets in the media pond. The stories, usually stuck on pages that are perused only by very thorough readers, certainly did not create the stir the subject deserved. Nonetheless, in her speech of 29 March, before the seven trawlers left for their sail of symbolic protest, the mayor of St. John's, Shannie Duff, had tried to suggest an analogy between the pillage of the cod and another bloody massacre that had used up much printer's ink for two decades. Duff invited Brigitte Bardot to clasp to her breast not a baby seal, but a cod, if she ever came back to Newfoundland, for the most threatened species was not the one she thought.

But how to evoke in the popular imagination the same protective, parental reflexes brought out by the puppy-like white-haired young seals, with their huge, limpid eyes, when the animal at stake is a cold-blooded fish with scaly, viscous skin and a face that is far from pretty, with its protruding, emotionless eyes and bloodless lips? Konrad Lorenz has clearly demonstrated, if not the impossibility of the task, at least the size of the challenge, in his *Studies of Animal and Human Behavior*. Such protective behaviour, he states, corresponds to instinctual impulses beyond all reason, since they are unleashed by the physiological features of the young. If this were not so, there would be no great difficulty in making the public understand that the seal hunt provoked passions only for aesthetic reasons. The disappearance of the cod and the other fishery resources is related to the more pressing problem of world hunger. But the cod are not likely to provoke protective behaviour, and so no one cares that they are being exterminated.

To catch the public's attention and the headlines, the overfishing issue would have to have a scandalous, atrocious, ignoble aspect. But there was none. In general, people expect fish to be fished: that is the normal course of things. The seas of Europe had been exploited to their extreme limit of yield long before the notions of environment and ecology were born in the collective conscience. Herring from the Baltic Sea have all but disappeared. Overfishing amounts to abuse—deplorable, of course—but not scandalous.

Although the plight of the northern cod was a case that could be pleaded to more sensitive spirits, it unfortunately lacked the sentimental aspect that would make it resonate in the public soul.

The strongly worded speeches by Clyde Wells, premier of Newfoundland, and Arthur Campeau, the Canadian prime minister's envoy to the United Nations, in New York in April of 1992, did not move international opinion any more than the reporters' stories had. The accusations of "environmental terrorism" and "high-seas piracy" launched by these two eminent Canadians against Spanish and Portuguese fishermen produced only a few lines in the foreign press. But since these speeches were delivered at preparatory meetings for the Earth Summit in Rio at the beginning of June, a kind of rehearsal really, it was hoped that their words would sound more of an alarm during the real performance, even though the fish issue would eventually be drowned in a veritable ocean of ecological causes.

More deplorably, the visit to Ottawa, at the beginning of May 1992, by Jacques Delors, the secretary general of the EC, and Cavaco Silva, the Portuguese prime minister, at the time serving his six-month term as president of the Community, provoked no demonstrations on Parliament Hill—not a hundred, not ten, or five, or even a single fisherman in oilskins and sou'wester brandishing a placard and fish bones, or something of the sort, turned up. The Canadian authorities all but rolled out the red carpet and deployed a guard of honour to welcome these dignitaries. Apparently, neither the NFFAWU nor the people from the government departments and the communications firm who had spared nothing in St. John's to show Newfoundlanders how concerned Ottawa was with their lot by inviting, informing, touring, and wining and dining dozens of journalists who would talk about them on the far side of the Atlantic, had seen—or understood—the golden opportunity presented by the visit of the two highest officers of the EC to dramatize the issue of overfishing.

Perhaps this would have been a breach in the rules of hospitality. On the other hand, hadn't ministers and senior Canadian bureaucrats been greeted with less-than-polite placards in Paris, London, and Amsterdam when the protest against the seal hunt was in full swing?

The absence of any demonstration left Delors and Silva with the impression that the issue of overfishing wasn't terribly important, even though the Canadian prime minister, Brian Mulroney, spent a significant part of their interview talking about it. Even worse, their visit left no image likely to impress television viewers here or in Europe—and, as we know, appearances are much more important than substance these days. Media diplomacy, too, missed the boat this time round!

This doesn't mean that the Ottawa's diplomatic approach bore no fruit. The government worked hard and made some progress, but it was confined to diplomatic arcana. During this time, the EC trawlers, along with fifteen vessels flying flags of convenience (Panama, South Korea), continued their genocide of the northern cod even in the spawning zones, while an international conference on the fisheries taking place in sunny Cancún deplored it.

Already there were rumours, circulating among the fronds of the coconut trees and in the cabañas, of the gloomy results of a NAFO study on the state of the northern cod stocks that was to be made public later. But Ted Anderson, who had left his seaside home, still in the grip of Labrador's ice, for the plush tropical environment, had no need of scientific studies. Again, he told people about the three cod caught the previous summer at Makkovik and about the urgency of addressing the issue before the day was over—and days ended much earlier in these latitudes.

For its part, our hastily formed environmental committee had quite a bit of trouble springing into action and spreading its message, because of both financial constraints and a lack of international credibility.

There is a flip side to ecology movements. Since they sprang up in the 1960s, following the cries of alarm raised by

Rachel Carson in *Silent Spring* and *The Sea Around Us*, they
have shown an annoying tendency to become multi-national
enterprises raking in huge sums of money (according to the
testimony of one of their spokespersons who appeared before
Judge Malouf's Royal Commission on the Seal Hunt); between a few of them, they have a sort of world monopoly on
environmental activism. For any organization that is not
under the umbrella of the Sierrra Club, the International
Fund for Animal Welfare, the Audubon Society, Greenpeace,
or one of a handful of others, it is practically impossible to
catch the attention of the global village, even for the best of
causes.

Our group's strategy thus consisted of establishing ties
with these powerful organizations. The Cree of James Bay,
the Florida panther, the Amazonian aboriginals, the whales,
the anti-nuclear issue, the elephants, and other such causes
are all listed in the catalogue of one or another. But since they
compete in a limited market, there is little doubt that considerations other than purely environmental ones sometimes
influence their choices. After all, these multinationals need
considerable funds to operate.

Now, as I've mentioned, *Gadus morhua* has two counts
against it: it isn't very cuddly, and it raises the question of the
uncontrolled proliferation of the very paradigm of ecological
causes: the Greenland seal. Clearly, Greenpeace, IFAW, and
the World Wildlife Fund wouldn't support a group that does
not share their views on the plight of these amphibians, on
which they had built their reputation—and some their
prosperity. Moreover, the cod crisis didn't have about it the
whiff of scandal essential to bringing great causes to light.
Fish, the food of penance, is spurned by more or less
everyone.

At the end of May, I received an emergency call from the
Department of External Affairs. It was a Friday at cocktail
hour, and I was being asked to leave my home in the Magdalen Islands the following day for St. John's to attend brief-
ings with a delegation of fishery representatives, of which I

was to be a member, heading for Scotland, France, Spain, and Portugal to plead the case of the cod. I recognized the same kind of last-minute approach that had been behind my trip to Newfoundland in March. I couldn't get to St. John's the next day; it was absolutely imposssible for me to get away before the following Tuesday, or Monday evening at the earliest.

That's okay, they said, so instead I was booked on an Air France flight leaving Mirabel Airport at five in the afternoon the following Tuesday, to meet up with the fishery delegation in Paris the next morning at eight at the Hôtel François Premier, on Rue Magellan. My itinerary had been organized with such brisk authority by the department that it seemed impossible to refuse.

After a quick shower at the hotel to recover from a night of interrupted sleep in the plane, I found the other six members of the delegation, fresh and rested, having had their breakfast of croissants and coffee, and ready to hop into the minibus for the nine-o'clock meeting at the Canadian embassy. They were Peter McCreath, Conservative Member of Parliament from Nova Scotia; George Baker, Liberal Member of Parliament from Newfoundland; David Stupich, New Democrat Member of Parliament from British Columbia; Senator Gerry Ottenheimer, from Newfoundland; Ron Bulmer, president of the Canadian Fisheries Council; and Leo Power, the group's consultant. The introductions were made very quickly, and I was left with a fog of names and faces and titles that I warned my companions it would take me a few days to assimilate. As we left the hotel, they told me that they had arrived in Paris the previous evening after visiting Aberdeen and Peterhead, Scotland. What they had seen in the fish-processing plants there—which, incidentally, were flying a Spanish flag—had profoundly shocked them.

As the minibus made its way through the narrow, busy, noisy streets of a city that seemed to me more suited for buggies than automobiles, someone added to the wad of papers I had received in the hall of the hotel a copy of the fax sent the previous evening to news agencies. I couldn't hear what he was saying because of the street noise, but I understood as he held up his index fingers to indicate length that he was talking about fish—and not the notorious expanding fish of anglers' stories, but shrinking ones, since his fingers drew together until they almost touched.

"That small!" he concluded indignantly.

And the others, shaking their heads, said that it was absolutely incredible, a true scandal!

15

The European Fishing Problems

IN THE CANADIAN EMBASSY we were handed a fax of the Canadian Press press release for the next day's newspapers: it was three o'clock in the morning on the other side of the Atlantic. The release said, in typically terse journalistic style:

Spanish ships are landing in Scotland "shocking" amounts of undersized cod caught off Canada's east coast, Newfoundland MP George Baker charged Tuesday.

Baker, who is touring Europe with a Canadian fisheries delegation, said his group has gathered proof on Spanish landings during a visit to the Aberdeen area over the past two days.

The group found that 70 per cent of cod landed by Spanish fishermen are less than 33 centimetres long—the European Community limit.

"This is alarming because the East Coast fisheries' only hope for the future is that these small fish will survive," Baker said in a telephone interview from Aberdeen after meeting Scottish fisheries officials.

"Now we see that the European Community allows the landing of drastically undersized fish as long as it's caught in Canadian waters," said Baker, Liberal member for Gander – Grand Falls.

Baker said that the evidence, including photographs, was collected during an inspection of several Scottish ports where cod is shipped to the large British fish market.

"If you landed such small fish in Newfoundland, you'd be arrested and thrown in prison," said Baker, adding that the Canadian cod limit is about 41 centimetres long.

The delegation of mainly East Coast MPs, fish producers and union leaders began a week-long sweep of eight EC countries in Scotland on Monday.

The 15-member group is seeking support against alleged overfishing by EC boats—especially from Spain and Portugal—just outside the Canadian 200-mile waters.

Canada says that the overfishing is destroying depleted cod stocks, the lifeblood of the ailing Atlantic Canada fishery. The EC has blamed the problem on Canadian boats.

In Aberdeen, Bob Allan, head of the Scottish Fishermen's Association, said he'll raise the issue with David Currie, Britain's fisheries minister.

Allen said the 6,000 members of his association—Scotland's largest fishermen's group—can understand the plight of Canadian fishermen.

Scottish fishermen have been hurt by overfishing by Spain and other countries in the North Sea. That's led to longer boat tie-ups and smaller fish quotas over the past few years.

Ron Bulmer, president of the Fisheries Council of Canada, which represents fish producers, said he was encouraged by the response of Scottish officials.

Bulmer said the "crunch" will come Thursday when he and the rest of the delegation start a four-day visit to fishing ports in Spain and Portugal.

"I'm not afraid of telling them to their face that they're the cause of our troubles," Bulmer said.

When they were in Peterhead and Aberdeen, around the plants flying the Spanish flag, Baker and Bulmer told me later, they saw containers of frozen fish being unloaded—tonnes and tonnes of it. In the containers were small, immature cod, of illegal size even according to European rules. They were barely bigger than tommycod or loaches.

The fact, revolting as it may be, they said, is that if these cod had been fished in European waters, they could not have been landed in Europe, on pain of a stiff fine. But, in a twist of hypocrisy, they *could* be landed in Europe if they had been caught elsewhere. The only place where they could conceivably have been caught was outside the Canadian E.E.Z., on the Nose of the Grand Banks or on the Flemish Cap.

Landing these catches in Scotland, three thousand kilometres from the fishing grounds, is a quick hop for modern freezer-trawlers, my companions said. What is most important for making these ships profitable is a certain density of fish, permitting a satisfactory daily catch rate. The distance to the landing port is a secondary factor.

As well, not all the containers came from the ships' holds, I was told. Some apparently arrived in Scotland by plane. George Baker had a theory on this subject, which could turn out to be an incredible story. But he didn't want to divulge it yet, because he had no proof. He intended to make use of our European tour to unearth it.

As we talked, we took our places in the conference room of the Canadian embassy in Paris. Then the ambassador, Claude T. Charland, made some helpful remarks on the French view of the issue. In France, he told us, the problem had two aspects. First, there was the dispute regarding territorial waters around Saint-Pierre and Miquelon, on which an arbitration court, selected by France and Canada, would render a final, no-appeal decision soon in New York. It was inappropriate to discuss this bilateral issue with our French interlocutors since it was before the court.

Then there was the question of EC overfishing, its refusal to comply with the NAFO quotas, and so on. In this Canada might find an unexpected ally in France, not only because the arbitration-court judgment could conceivably establish some sort of partnership between France and Canada regarding certain fish stocks (not precisely what happened, as it turned out), but also because French president François Mitterand had seemed very interested in the explanation of the situation presented to him by Prime Minister Mulroney when he was in Paris. More than a quarter of the meeting between Mitterand and Mulroney, which Charland had attended, dealt with the question (this is enormous, by diplomatic standards). Mitterand had taken a long look at the charts and the computerized images, which resembled abstract paintings, prepared by Canadian scientists to show the extent of overfishing and stock depletion.

Besides, the fact that Canada accused mainly Spain and Portugal of overfishing could not help but trigger France's sympathy, for France had its own share of frictions with its southern neighbours with regard to sharing the fishing zones. They had had to fire cannons in the Gulf of Gascogne that very spring to drive Spanish fishing vessels out of their zone.

As to other matters, we were advised not to raise the issue of the uncontrolled proliferation of Greenland seals, since this was still a very hot topic in France. On the other hand, a good subject for discussion was the increased danger of whales beaching, since, with fewer fish, they are forced to feed closer and closer to the coasts, as biologist Dan Goodman, of Fisheries and Oceans Canada, had observed. This was the type of bait that the French rose to.

In his office at the *Assemblée nationale*—the luxurious Second Empire furniture and the tapestries on the walls greatly impressed his Canadian counterparts—Jean Beaufils, Socialist member for Dieppe and Seine-Maritime, and a close associate of French Minister of Fisheries Josselin, also deplored the destructive effects of overfishing. He knew what the Canadian delegation was talking about, since in recent years France had had to face a painful reduction in its fishing effort due to the scarcity of fish.

The industry seemed incapable of restraining itself anywhere, he told us. It was common knowledge that the quota for anchovies in the Gulf of Gascogne (3,000 tonnes) was already too high, yet the fishermen from southern Europe didn't care: they exceeded it by large amounts year after year.

"The Spanish, Portuguese, and Italian fishermen don't respect the Community rules with regard to fish," Beaufils continued. "We have great difficulty with this. It's a source of friction between our countries." And then he told us about the intervention of the French gunship against Spanish anchovy-fishing boats in the Gulf of Gascogne.

The European Community's main problem is policing its fishing fleets, he said. According to agreements among the twelve member countries, only inspectors from each respective country are authorized to board the ships in the Community's common fishing zones (not to be confused with each country's territorial waters). These all but powerless inspectors can inspect the catch reports, but not the hold. Infractions, if any can be found under these circumstances , are referred to the country of the transgressor, to which it then falls to apply the sanctions provided in Community law. When such infractions are in fact referred to them, the courts have a tendency to be lenient with their compatriots.

Nevertheless, the EC is aware of the overfishing, not only in the northwest Atlantic, but also on its side of the ocean, Beaufils added. To remedy this, it has adopted a Multi-Year Orientation Plan (MOP), which aims to diminish the catching power of member countries. For France, this has meant reducing the power of its fleet by 10 per cent between 1987 and 1992. A new five-year plan being discussed in Brussels will require further reductions of France and other countries. Generally, although it follows different modalities, the MOP functions similarly in all EC countries and requires them to retire from their fleets, vessels more than ten years old. Compensation is provided to owners for voluntarily destroying their ships, as is aid with selling them, notably to Africa, or for converting them for other activities.

"It's hard for someone who has made his living with his ship to let go of it," Beaufils said. "We've seen more than one old sailor shed a tear when he let his ship go."

If a country does not attain the objectives fixed by the MOP, it is disqualified from receiving grants offered by the EC for, ironically, naval construction, which, added to other national and regional grants, can amount to 50 per cent of the cost of building new fishing units. Without them, Beaufils told us, it would be impossible to run the shipyards.

The disturbing corollary to this carrot-and-stick policy is clear: in parallel to the reduction of its catching power, measured in horsepower, Europe is pursuing a vigorous policy of fleet modernization. It is fairly obvious that the hoped-for effects of the first objective can be annulled or, at least, attenuated by the second. It must also be noted that there is a troubling gap in this legislation: a country can easily subtract one unit from its fleet and continue to have it fish under a different flag. Many in Canada strongly suspect Spain and Portugal of using countries such as Panama and South Korea to reflag their old ships. Technically, they have got rid of their excess catching power and are eligible for European grants. But in fact nothing has changed. Fifteen percent of foreign ships fishing outside the limit of Canadian waters fly flags of convenience.

Another measure adopted by the EC to protect the resource is increasing mesh size, which, up to recently, was not regulated. Fishermen used the net that they considered appropriate. Trawl pockets could have mesh of 80 mm, or sometimes even 60 mm.

Although many fishermen argue that the size of the mesh has only a minor influence on the size of fish caught (once the "large" fish—skates and so on—obstruct the net, the small ones cannot escape), it is generally admitted that larger meshes reduce the catch of small fish—that is, juvenile individuals. In Europe, the short-term aim is to generalize the use of whiting nets, with 90-mm mesh, and in the medium term to bring the limit to 110 mm, which would still be below Canada's standard of 135 mm.

But in Europe as in Canada, it is very difficult to make sure that the mesh-size limit is respected. Many trawler fishermen, even Canadian ones, sew into their legal-mesh pocket a lining with smaller mesh, which they can take out when a suspect ship (inspection or other) shows up on their radar screen. With these powerful instruments, which can "see" 30 nautical miles and more, there is plenty of time to remove the illegal lining before they are boarded.

Anyway, according to the EC protocols, on-board inspections are impossible. The size of the mesh can be checked only at dockside, after the ship has returned to its home port. The end result is the massacre of small cod observed in Scotland.

There was silence when Mr. Baker, M.P. for Gander– Grand Falls, Newfoundland, brought this up again in the swank office of Mr. Beaufils, representative from Dieppe, the fifth-largest fishing port in France in terms of volume of landings (fine species: turbot, sole, and scallops).

But in France too, Beaufils informed us, the fisheries are in jeopardy. He promised to convey Canada's complaints to the Minister of Fisheries, who would in turn exert his influence at the European Commission, since this body has the final word. As someone from Dieppe, he said, it was the very least he could do for Canada.

Dieppe, where Canadian soldiers had been sacrificed by the thousands in the failed landing of August, 1942. It was inevitable that the interview ended on this note, evoking the fraternity between two nations.

A little later, in Le Bourbonnais, where the Canadian embassy offered a luncheon meeting with journalists, my neighbour at the table brought me up to date on the decision structures of the EC and the relationships that exist among European nations.

He told me that within the EC there is a north-south problem analogous, in a proportional way, to the worldwide social cleavage. Greece, Spain, and Portugal are less economically developed than England, Germany, Benelux, and France, and fishing represents a higher percentage of the GNP in these countries. Decisions made in Brussels must take account of this, and thus Spain and Portugal in particular have more say in the various agencies that regulate fishing. This is not codified in black and white, my neighbour hastened to add, but it is how things in fact happen.

France's influence over decisions reached by the EC must be seen in this perspective. And it must not be forgotten, although it isn't trumpeted far and wide, that the unilateral allocation by the EC of generous quotas to, mainly, Portugal and Spain in the NAFO zones bordering Canadian waters eases internal tensions between fishing countries of the EC in its own waters. As they say, it takes a thorn from the lion's paw!

When dessert was over, we shook hands with the French journalists, who promised that the public in their country would be alerted to the European fleets' savage assault on the Canadian northern cod. Then we climbed into the minibus and drove to Charles de Gaulle Airport for our flight to Madrid, through bottlenecks, traffic jams, and the congestion that is second nature to Paris, especially on the eve of the long Ascension Day weekend.

As we travelled, George Baker (I was now beginning to match up the names and faces of my companions) took some papers out of his ever-present briefcase. They were photocopies of tenders made by various trawlers that were fishing on the Nose of the Grand Banks, which he had found at the Aberdeen and Peterhead plants. They described the catch, with a corresponding price for each category: so much cod of such and such a size, so much of another size, so much plaice, and so on. All revealed abominably high percentages (60 to 70 per cent) of juvenile cod of a size clearly below European standards.

Multiplying the trend that appeared in these documents by the hundred or so ships that sweep up the fish makes one dizzy. This is not simple overfishing, but extermination, a true slaughter: not only because by taking fish so small one kills an infinitely higher number of individuals per tonne caught than one would of larger fish, but also because all these cod will never have a chance to reproduce. In effect, it mortgages the future of the Newfoundland fisheries right up to the beginning of the next millennium.

The problem, as Ron Bulmer framed it, is that it is impossible for these ships to stop fishing without causing insoluble financial problems. The ruthless requirements of the money market, the interest rates, and the dividends paid to investors require them to continue destroying the stocks—blindly, since shortage will hit soon or later; even an idiot can see this.

But the law of the market, the lifeblood of the current world economic paradigm, seems not to allow for even this modicum of foresight.

On the jammed expressway, the minibus wove its way between growling vans and cars, while motorcycles scuttled and whined like insects in the narrow gaps in the traffic.

Modern city life is an exercise in shuttling people in in the morning and shuttling them out in the evening, through dense rush-hour traffic and air full of exhaust fumes. Within the scale of importance that Western humans attribute above all to themselves and to their material comfort, this reproduces the work of sponges, very primitive forms of life, as everyone knows.

However, it is from these city-organisms, in which people find themselves reduced to the role of a sort of functional globule, a human fuel, that are secreted almost everything that affects the rest of the planet. Without the urban way of life, with all it means in terms of artifice and spoilage of nature, with its industrial-strength consumption of just about everything and pollution, even of the soul, as its by-product, the planetary environment would no doubt be much better off.

Most troubling of all is that people in the cities, dissociated from nature as they are, impose their ideas about ecology on the rest of the world.

16

"No sera nada por nadie"

THE NEXT DAY, IN MADRID, we worried that Ascension Day, the day of a general strike in Spain, might upset our schedule. However, the Spanish were at pains to impress the Canadian fisheries delegation.

The first item on the schedule was a visit to the *Camara de Comercio y Industria de Madrid*, located in the old residence of the Marquis of Monzanedo, also Duke of Santona: Carrara marble stairs, gold-leafed woodwork, colonnades, walls and ceilings covered with works of art, sculptures and cherubs in the niches, tapestries, and crystal chandeliers—enough to flabbergast those of us, who, the previous day in Paris, had found Mr. Beaufils's office luxurious.

In the oval drawing-room, or boudoir, with such sensitive acoustics that someone at the centre of the ellipse did not have to raise his voice to be heard by all, *Señor* Miguel Cachot, from the Chamber's External Commerce and International Relations Commission, received us with exquisite politeness. He lent an attentive ear to our group's complaints and sympathized with our anxieties regarding the disastrous effect of overfishing the cod stocks. The Spanish would be the first to suffer, he mentioned in passing, since they are among the largest consumers of marine products on the planet.

After these courteous exchanges in the duchess's drawing-room, we had a tour of the rest of the house, splendidly restored in its original style, which achieved the impression of grandeur that our hosts no doubt wanted to instill in our minds. Here, from each mahogany veneer, from each carved moulding, from each mural of hunt scenes or of *geishas* at the market, the history and culture of a people contemplated us, subtly reinforcing the message that precisely what we lack, in the New World, to back certain of our claims is the legitimacy that a secular historical heritage bestows.

This was also the gist of the remark made later by Excelentísimo Jose Loira Rúa, general secretary of maritime fisheries, from the Spanish Department of Agriculture, Fisheries, and Food. He stated categorically that Spain possesses historical fishing rights on the Grand Banks of Newfoundland. And much older than those of Canada, he had the delicacy not to add explicitly, aware, as he shot a proud look at each member of our delegation, that this was precisely what we were thinking.

Loira Rúa had returned from a meeting of the EC's Fisheries Commission in Brussels specifically to meet with us. This bespoke the importance he placed on our visit, stated his colleague, Rafael Conde de Saro, director general of fishing resources, in perfect English. The son of a diplomat, Conde de Saro lived for years in Canada and attended McGill University. However, he seemed as impervious as his superior to our allegations of overfishing, pronounced in an elegant Spanish by Senator Ottenheimer, who speaks five languages. Loira Rúa, his suit a bit rumpled, his tie loosened (in accord with the socialist image), with a full beard and glasses, was the image of the active, ardent technocrat. Obviously, we weren't likely to hear expressions of guilt from him. I saw him energetically shake his head to each complaint translated by the interpreter, as the other members of our delegation embellished on Senator Ottenheimer's statements.

"I appreciate at least the tone in which these remarks are made," Loira Rúa said when it was his turn to speak. But he refuted each point, one after the other. He argued that Spain is not guilty of overfishing in Canadian waters, and he cited statistics (numbers, types of ship, catches, etc.) to illustrate the reduction of the Spanish fishing effort over the past twenty years. In the 1970s, 106 *pareas* (trawlers fishing in pairs) were raking the floor of the Grand Banks (I had seen a few of them when I was on board the *Cape Freels*). There were only twenty-two of them now. As well, the Spanish scientists were not warning of a collapse of the resource that would justify stopping fishing.

Conde de Saro nodded his head approvingly.

Loira Rúa did not deny that there was a drop in stocks. But the east coast of Canada was not the only region affected, he added. In Spain also, it caused problems: ten thousand jobs had been lost in the fisheries sector in recent years. And with the way things were going, the future did not look much brighter for the Spanish fishing communities than for those of Newfoundland. Whose fault was it? Poor management, surely, proposed the senior civil servant. At the same time as it was scaling down cod allocations for foreign fleets within its exclusive two-hundred-mile zone at the beginning of the 1980s, had Canada not authorized wild overfishing of the banks by its own inshore and offshore fishing fleets? Did it think that Spain would sit quietly by while its historical rights were being flouted?

But, in his opinion, intensive fishing was not the sole cause of the decline in stocks, Loira Rúa hastened to add; not enough attention was paid to the effect of factors such as climatic change and the general degradation of the marine environment on the abundance of fishing resources; as well, without a global approach to the ecosystem, dangerous predator–prey imbalances develop.

"*Las focas,*" he pronounced. The seals. All the members of the Canadian delegation nodded in agreement. But what did Spain plan to do about the issue of the EC ban on importation of seal products? I asked. The two bureaucrats looked at each other, and gave a noncommital response.

For the Spanish, I learned later, it's not so simple: taking a position in favour of the seal hunt would result in raising yet again the issue of their national sport, bullfighting. It is high on the list of targets of bleeding-heart ecologists from northern Europe, especially the English, who wanted, if not total abolition, at least the end of killing the bull before the crowd.

What struck me the most, as the conversation went on, was Spain's deep suspicion of Canada with regard to fishing. There was in the attitude of our Spanish interlocutors something incredulous and ironic that seemed to signal that they impugned ulterior motives to our mission, though they were too polite to say so outright. In fact, although the Canadian embassy had reassured them a hundred times on this subject, they still thought that Canada intended to extend its exclusive economic zone to 350 miles from the coast in order to have total control of its cod resources.

This is a ludicrous notion to anyone who knows how difficult it is for Canada, with its scant resources, to conduct surveillance and policing actions within its two-hundred-mile zone; such actions would be even more ridiculously symbolic in a maritime expanse 75 per cent larger. But it was not obvious to the Spanish. Had not the extension of Canada's territorial waters to two hundred miles signified the eviction of foreign codfishing fleets during the 1980s, in spite of the oft-repeated reassurances by the Canadian Minister of Fisheries that he did not want to "starve the rest of the world"?

At the heart of the problem lay the issue of confidence. The more Canada awaited a positive gesture from Spain, the more Spain expected one from Canada—like, as our hosts suggested, the reopening of Canadian ports to their ships— which Canada refused in order not to lose the only leverage it had on Spain, even though this deprived port cities of the revenues that foreign ships would bring in.

Loira Rúa then announced that Spain had decided to make the opening move. As of the first of June, two days hence, it would withdraw its fleet from zone 2J3KL, the Nose of the Grand Banks. This was a scoop, he told us, with the flourish of a matador soliciting applause from the crowd, for it had just been decided in Brussels, and it would of course affect the entire EC fleet.

But, instead of the enthusiastic reception he expected, our delegation had mixed reactions. Of course, the gesture was appreciated, as was the official spin with which it was presented, which stressed the importance of the issue. However, anyone with knowledge of the Grand Banks fisheries would be well aware that at this time of year, the cod have moved closer to the coasts in pursuit of the capelin, and are thus well within the Canadian zone. There are not enough in international waters for profitable fishing by the huge oil-hungry units of the foreign fleets. Unless the fleets were recalled to their respective home ports, Spain's gesture would be just window dressing, and no one on our side of the table was buying it.

In fact, to questions dealing with redistribution of their fishing units (wouldn't they in fact just be removed from the Nose of the Grand Banks and sent to the Tail—zone 3N, to take flat fish? suggested George Baker), our Spanish hosts responded only very vaguely, simply repeating that their ships would leave 2J3KL on the first of June—and wasn't that what we Canadians wanted?

As the interview drew to a close, the question of catching immature cod, such as those in the containers landed at Aberdeen, had to be addressed. Our Spanish hosts vehemently disclaimed any responsibility, blaming the Portuguese or ships flying flags of convenience. Spain, they said, was not interested in taking such small fish, because the Spanish market is for salt fish, which requires larger cod. Therefore, another country must be the culprit.

However, we told them, we had copies of telegraphed tenders made by Spanish trawlers, among others, to the Scottish plants in Aberdeen, and there was also the matter of that Spanish flag floating over the plants where cod under 30 cm in length were being processed. Loira Rúa and Conde de Saro denied all of this with vigorous head shakes. Weren't their fishing ships using nets with a mesh size of 100 mm, which lets the small fish pass through? If they learned that small cod were being taken deliberately, they would certainly intervene, and harshly. They claimed to be in absolute agreement with Canada that this was indeed a scandal.

Between sessions, waiting to meet with members of the parliamentary commission on fisheries and agriculture, we toured the Spanish parliament, the domed ceiling of which still carried traces of the bullets from the failed coup attempt of 1981. Baker and Bulmer were trying to figure out exactly what the withdrawal of the Spanish fleet from zone 2J3KL meant; they concluded that it was a show without real substance, for the Spanish fisheries did not lose anything in the end. Baker was still wondering how the small cod got to the Spanish plants in Scotland. Of course, some freezer-trawlers crossed the 3,500 kilometres of the Atlantic to deliver them, but not every fishing unit could do this. There had to be a link somewhere, and he wanted to know where it was. For their part, Peter McCreath, Senator Ottenheimer, and Canada's ambassador to Spain, Jean-Pierre Juneau, were considering the diplomatic implications of the just-announced Spanish moratorium. This was the first time that Spain had made the slightest concession to Canada with regard to the fishery, Juneau emphasized; even if it was purely symbolic, it had to be considered an encouraging first move. To belittle it would be a great insult to this immensely proud people, and would perhaps close the door to the search for a common solution for many years to come.

Spain is subject to formidable constraints in its fishing activities, we learned when we met the members of the Royal Parliamentary Commission on the Fisheries. Although it has the largest fishing fleet of any EC country, it also has among the fewest resources. It is deprived of an exclusive coastal zone on the Atlantic by Portugal, which occupies the southwest part of the Iberian peninsula, and by France, with which it must share the Gulf of Gascogne; as well, it shares its Mediterranean waters with Morocco and Algeria—although the Mediterranean Sea is suffocating from pollution and there are almost no fish left in it. Its possession of the Canary Islands, from which one of the Commission members was a deputy, gives it some fishing rights along the African coast; however, it has to share these with Morocco. Only its world-scale fishing operations, technological innovations, such as trawling to 1,400 metres in depth, and expertise in processing and marketing species not previously thought of as commercial enable Spain to maintain itself among the largest fishing countries.

Two regions of Spain in particular are responsible for the country's fishing: the Basque and Galicia, where the three largest fishing ports in Europe are found.

Galicia, the next stop on our tour, is a mountainous region where the humid Atlantic winds make rain an almost daily phenomenon. Twenty thousand people there are inshore fishermen, and ten thousand more are involved in the offshore fishery and processing. Ten percent of the economy depends on the fishery, which represents 40 percent of added value in this autonomous region of of the kingdom.

In the large meeting room of the Xunta Galicia Executive Council, at Santiago de Compostela, Dr. Enrique-Cesar Lopez Veiga, fisheries and aquaculture advisor (full beard à la Castro, a high scientist's forehead, thick glasses behind which glinted intelligent, mobile eyes), began by saying that Galicians are not known for their humility. They are Celts with an enduring patriotism and pride. Galicia is an autonomous region, with its own language and government, which, however, has limited power; an appreciable part of the electorate, represented by the Bloc National in their parliament, would like it to be a fully independent state. Although it does not have constitutional jurisdiction over offshore fishing or international matters, it has powerful political leverage and can exert a major influence on the Madrid government and, through it, on the European bureaucracy.

"We don't like arrogance," said Lopez Veiga. And, in the view of Galicians, Canada's attitude regarding other fishing countries was nothing less than arrogant: arrogant because Spain's cod quotas were cut within the E.E.Z. even after they conformed to certain catch reductions at the beginning of the 1980s; because of the closure of Canadian ports to foreign fishing ships since 1986 in retaliation for their overfishing on the Nose and Tail of the Grand Banks; and finally—to this Lopez Veiga, with a doctorate in biology, was particularly sensitive—because the Canadian scientists were not sharing the fruit of their research with other fishing countries. The biometric data gathered within the Canadian two-hundred-mile zone, according to this high executive in the Galician fishery, was treated almost like a state secret, making a comprehensive assessment of cod populations difficult for the Spanish, since they migrate from inside to outside the zone, and Spanish scientists can conduct studies only in the latter area.

For all of these reasons, said Lopez Veiga, "we defend our right to fish outside Canada's two-hundred-mile limit and do not recognize the privileges of any one country. We have chosen to be what I call active pessimists. It is true that we are using our European unilateral TAC as a political weapon, but Canada has left us no choice."

Now, Lopez Veiga recalled the negotiations started in 1981 by Canada with Spain and Portugal for a progressive reduction in the fishing effort of the latter two countries in Canadian waters over a ten-year period, leading to an end to their fishing in the northwest Atlantic by 1991. The negotiations had failed, after coming within a hair's breadth of succeeding, when Canada, under pressure from the heads of large fisheries companies, changed its mind and didn't sign the agreement. These company heads, with a nationalist sentiment exacerbated by the atmosphere prevailing at the time of the Kirby Report, wanted to keep for themselves all the cod that they thought (mistakenly) were so abundant. In the end, their greediness didn't get them much. For the Spanish, imbued with their historical rights, this had been a bitter pill to swallow.

But all of this was in the past, Lopez Veiga conceded. The situation must be looked at in terms of the present predicament. Canada has never been very sensitive to Spain's problems with regard to fishing. However, there would be much to gain through greater understanding and cooperation, rather than through confrontation. Canada could also benefit from the Galicians' expertise, notably with regard to the processing and marketing of ocean products.

One day, Lopez Veiga concluded, Canada would be the only one to exploit its cod resources. This was inevitable over the long term. But between now and then, Spain must not be expected to relinquish what it considered to be its right. The policies of all parties must necessarily display an attitude of openness and reconciliation, or else *"no sera nada por nadie"*—there will be nothing left for anyone.

17

The Massacre of the Baby Cod

FROM SANTIAGO DE COMPOSTELA to Vigo, a hundred kilometres of road winds through the mountains, past sycamore forests and small villages of stone houses surrounded with grapevines. As we approached the port town, the river and then the estuary were full of mussel-growing rafts.

"With the water temperature here," Ron Bulmer told me, "you can grow a commercial-size mussel in nine months, while it takes two years on the east coast of Canada."

The hundred or so giant trawlers moored in the port, as well as the sign on a tavern saying *Taberna Terra-Nova*, bear witness to the primary vocation of the town. From here, the Flemish Cap is only 1,500 nautical miles away.

We had a meeting with fishery industrialists in the buildings of *El Canal de Experiencias Pesqueras de Vigo*. They did not seem to be unduly upset by the alarming state of the resource as described to them by biologist Ray Bowring, once with Fisheries and Oceans Canada and now employed by Fisheries Product International. The levels of cod populations are the lowest ever observed, he told them, between half and a third of what they were only two years ago. Eighteen months before, the biomass of the northern cod was estimated at a million tonnes; today, it was evaluated at no more than 500,000 to 750,000 tonnes; two-thirds of this biomass comprised individuals from the 1989–90 recruitment, that is, very young cod, well under the age of sexual maturity. It was feared that if the fishing continued, given the very low level of mature individuals, there would be a rupture in the stock for the 1996 and 1997 age classes.

The gentlemen on the other side of the table listened closely, acquiescing with nods of their heads to certain statements and refuting others by shaking their heads energetically. But they never stopped smiling, even when they were facing the worst accusations of overfishing.

When it was their turn to speak, their spokesperson said that they shared Canada's fears with regard to the eventual decline of the resource. Their country hoped to fish for a long time to come in the waters of the northwest Atlantic, and the situation concerned them greatly. However, it was difficult for them to think that this decline, if decline there was, could be attributed to unconsidered fishing on their part. After all, Spain had expertise in fishing that few other countries could boast, Canada included. As for the rest, wasn't Canada refusing to take part in an international scientific debate on the issue of the Grand Banks resources?

There was indignation in his tone: did we think that the EC was acting totally irresponsibly when it granted itself unilateral quotas in the Grand Banks zone? Was it not reasonable to believe that the EC had done this because its own scientific studies indicated that it could? After all, how could the EC, which was exploiting only 10 per cent of the area of the Grand Banks, wreak more havoc than Canada, which controlled 90 per cent?

According to European scientific studies, he added, one could not deduce that the decline in the cod populations is attributable to overfishing. Other factors enter into the equation: ice, fish migrations, degradation of the environment, the uncontrolled increase in Greenland seals, which affects the capelin on which the cod feed, and so on. Starting up the whale hunt again after the international moratorium expired should be considered in order to diminish the pressure on the capelin, he said. But, of course, this decision would be made by the Brussels Commision.

Everyone around him concurred, especially when he invoked Europe and placed the entire question of overfishing under its protective shield. He wanted us to understand that they, the fisheries owners, the shipowners, Galicia, and Spain, in the end, all acted within a framework defined by the EC, which legitimized their actions.

Don't think for a minute, added the manager of the off-shore fleet (a man with huge shoulders and hands, whom I suspected was more at ease in a sweater with an anchor embroidered on it than in his suit and tie), that the EC exercises no control over his fleets. It places observers on board a certain number of ships, he said, and the ships are submitted to NAFO inspections, even if Europe does not agree with its catch quotas. Moreover, Madrid inspectors check the landings even here, in Vigo. It is far from the truth, he said, that all of these activities are not closely monitored.

The truly guilty parties were the trawlers flying flags of convenience, he said, who took 8,000 tonnes of cod, against 42,000 for the entire EC. These were the true rapists! The outlaws! These pirates had to be driven out of the fishery! And everyone roundly denounced these marauders, countries without pride or honour, which sold their flag for a few dollars: Panama, South Korea, and the others.

The members of our delegation might have joined the chorus, except that one let slip that a number of these ships were in fact often old European units reflagged (which permitted the concerned companies to include them in their allocation of reduction in catching power), and that they were strongly suspected of continuing to fish for their original countries.

When the question of fishing the small cod processed in the Scottish plants flying the Spanish flag was raised, the reaction of the fisheries heads was disconcerting. Instead of the concerned air that the other Spanish representatives to whom we had spoken had adopted, they looked at each other and began to laugh, as if it were a good joke.

"It is certainly not the Spanish who are doing that," said the one who had up to then conducted most of the discussion. "The Danes, perhaps. They are the ones who take small fish to make fish meal, which they use to fatten up their pigs. Or maybe the flags of convenience . . ."

Of course.

"No, no, no," interrupted George Baker. "They are Spanish and Portuguese trawlers. We've seen sales tenders telegraphed to the plants. And then, there are the containers that arrive by air, full of beheaded, gutted, frozen cod. Where could they come from? Saint-Pierre and Miquelon?" he ventured.

There was silence on the other side of the table, then a protest arose that was perhaps too vehement to be sincere: "No, no. Certainly not from Saint-Pierre and Miquelon!"

"Gentlemen, gentlemen!" cut in one of the industrialists with a noble, haughty air who had not said anything up to now. "We are wasting time politely telling one another very unpleasant things. This is not the time for useless recriminations. Instead of discussing the problems, we should use our time to come up with solutions."

As he talked, he gestured with his hands, as Italians do, turning elegant phrases full of sparkling wit and intelligence, and he soon had everyone under his spell. Spain had the fishing expertise, Canada had the resource, he said: a partnership between the two countries would seem obvious. The future could only be in joint ventures, in cooperation rather than confrontation.

In fact, he continued, forms of protectionism such as two-hundred-mile exclusive economic zones had run their course—and had proved their inefficiency. With globalization of economies, the fisheries must be managed on a world-wide scale: close collaboration between Canada and Europe in this regard would be a constructive example for the rest of the world. And so on.

This was a philosophy diametrically opposed to Canada's, which is based on the privileges accorded to coastal states by the Law of the Sea for management of species whose habitat fall within its exclusive zone in whole or in part. Nevertheless, some in our delegation seemed to agree with the Spaniards' proposals.

In the bus on the way back to Santiago de Compostela, I remarked on this to a member of our delegation. He told me that some fishing companies in Newfoundland and the Maritimes were already doing business with the Spanish. "A few of them are actually doing business with the guys who were sitting across the table just now."

Then, as we drove through the forests of sycamores that were shedding bark in the humid underbrush, I thought of Ted Anderson, on his Labrador rock, in Makkovik, of him and his three cod caught in the nets the summer before, where the trawlers had caught millions of kilos a few years earlier. Was this, then, the ineluctable destiny of the fisheries in the global economy, that its principal antagonism would express itself, beyond international frictions, between inshore and offshore fishermen, between the artisan and industry? Those for whom the fate of the fish is gauged in exclusively financial terms and those for whom it is a way of life?

The next day, we saw what the Spanish really meant by expertise in fishing when we visited one of the three canneries of Escuris, a company that processes and markets a wide variety of products world-wide in all formats required by the market. Tuna, sardines, mackerel, cockles, clams, razor clams, mussels, squid, octopus, eel, cod roe, scombrioids, and so on, were preserved in oil, *escabeche*, tomato sauce, marinara sauce, with lemon, with garlic, with pimentos, and sent all over the world. Anyone familiar with Canada's extreme clumsiness at processing its sea products would be stunned by the immense size of the plant, especially when he remembers all the mackerel that fishermen who come in a little late in the evening have to throw back into the sea because the producer has reached his freezer capacity, or if he knows about the tonnes of herring that ended up in the Yarmouth dump a few years ago, because no one knew what to do with them once the Japanese had taken the roe to send back to their country for further processing!

The Escuris plants are supplied by the local fishermen and fish farmers and by ships fishing around the world. Thanks to a computerized system, they know, for instance, when a tuna ship will arrive from the faraway Seychelle Islands, and can plan production accordingly. In the huge work rooms, the size of several football fields, a network of slings, chains, bridges, and conveyor belts controlled by the latest technology, routes different products from the filleters, slicers, and kettles to packaging, in one gigantic continuous motion. Again thanks to computers, any particular lot of cans can be tracked through all processing stages.

But there is more to the plant than advanced technology. The employees' rest areas and cafeteria are comfortable and pleasant. Hung on the walls are large paintings by local artists, works of figurative and abstract art, portraying the ocean, the marine world, and fishing, as if to give work in the plant a significance beyond simply earning one's living, melding with the milieu, the culture, the very spirit of the people.

In the manager's office—leather couches, carved mahogany furniture—where we were served coffee, juice, wine, and Escuris hors d'oeuvres, there were also large paintings on the walls. At the back of the room stood a set of large glass-fronted bookshelves, perhaps similar to those found in some managers' offices at Canadian fishery companies. I didn't pay much attention to it, since I was busy admiring the art. But Senator Ottenheimer, a distinguished philologist, invited me to take a closer look. On one shelf, well within reach, there were a half-dozen volumes bound in calfskin and titled in gold leaf: the complete works of Miguel de Cervantes.

"Do you know many Canadian fishing-company managers," he asked me with a smile, "who have the complete works of Shakespeare in their offices?"

In the meantime, George Baker was tirelessly pursuing his inquiry into how the small, immature Grand Banks baby cod had ended up at the Aberdeen plants. For him, the tour was turning into a sort of detective story. He missed no opportunity to talk with people who could provide clues, which he checked in the evenings during transatlantic phone calls. The previous evening, at the *Canal de Experiencias Pesqueras de Vigo*, I had seen him in long conversation with the gentleman who had spoken last.

In the train that took us to Porto, Portugal, Baker told me that he had found the key to the puzzle. It turned out that this man was part of the Spanish consortium that had acquired 70 per cent of the shares in the Inter-Pêche fish-processing plant in Saint-Pierre and Miquelon, and he had supplied the missing links.

Cod fished in the waters adjacent to the Canadian E.E.Z. were indeed landed at Saint-Pierre. They were summarily dressed, gutted, beheaded, and frozen, then packed in containers, which, duly sealed, were sent by ferry and road to St. John's, Newfoundland. There, they were loaded onto one of the two or three weekly Air Canada flights to Scotland. Thus, the immature cod plundered on the Nose of the Grand Banks literally passed under Canada's nose on their way to British consumers. Canadian customs could not intercept the sealed containers without provoking a diplomatic scandal even more resounding than that of the extermination of the "baby" cod.

But, in spite of the revolting aspects of the operation, the business sense of those who perpetrated it was undeniable. Worth 24 cents a pound landed at Saint-Pierre and $1.24 when they arrive at the Scotland plants, with transportation costs added, these very small cod are still marketed at a satisfying profit. Two minuscule fillets, too small to be deboned and together weighing from seventy to seventy-five grams, are coated with 50 per cent of their weight in deep-frying batter to make a portion of fish and chips for which British consumers willingly pay a pound sterling and more. As for the bones, which would make such a product utterly unmarketable in North America, they don't bother the British, who consume five to six times more fish than we do every year. They simply spit the bones out, as they've been doing for centuries!

Of course, it doesn't occur to British consumers that they are participating in the depletion of a resource that is, if not threatened, at least in peril. After all, who can identify a "baby cod" under half a centimetre of batter?

As the train sliced through the black expanse beside the ocean in the Portuguese night, I couldn't stop reflecting on the irony of it all. Unable to slip through the illegal small-sized meshes that stopped them from escaping the trawls in the first place, the small cod fished outside Canada's E.E.Z. slipped through the EC regulations forbidding the catch of fish that small in its own waters, and their plants from purchasing it. Since they came from elsewhere, they could be eaten, legally and in good conscience, by the Brits. It remained to be seen if the British, who made such a row over the hunt of "baby" seals, would, in the interest of fairness, rise up with the same vigour against the lot of the poor "baby" cod.

I spent my twenty-hour stopover in London, between Portugal and Canada, phoning journalists on the environment beat for all the large dailies, to bring them up to date on the crusty fish-and-chips affair. To each one, I mentioned the parallel between the slaughter of the "baby" cod and that of the "baby" seals, which had raised such a ruckus in their country. Time after time, I pointed out and stressed forcefully that for the seals, whose populations had been growing despite the hunt, the question was solely one of aesthetics, and most agreed, while for the cod, the collapse in population of which was no less than catastrophic, it was an issue connected to world hunger.

One thing about the English: they are courteous. The reporters listened, and most of them recognized that there was indeed a real and thorny problem. It is, indeed, all the greater a problem for them, since they are such great fish consumers that they happily substitute boiled kipper for bacon with their breakfast.

But unless one is backed up by the major players in environmental activism, a campaign like this is condemned after only a few telephone calls. There is no photo of the star of the hour in a wetsuit clasping a baby cod to her breast, and no money. And it has even less a chance for success if one is asking those who are principally responsible for the situation to cast the first stone.

If my approach got a few paragraphs, they were discreetly burried in the back pages, like the other coverage of overfishing by the EC, beside the classified ads and the obituaries.

18

The Bottom of the Barrel

AFTER OUR EUROPEAN TOUR, the final, no-appeal judgment of the New York tribunal on the question of the territorial waters of Saint-Pierre and Miquelon confirmed the worst fears of George Baker, the Newfoundland M.P. By a majority of three to two (the dissidents, ironically, being France and Canada), the tribunal gave France an exclusive zone of twenty-four miles around its archipelago, as well as a narrow corridor, ten and a half miles wide and more than two hundred miles long, linking it to international waters through Canada's E.E.Z.

Although it is of negligible importance for fishing, since it cuts through only the small Green Banks, slightly west of the Grand Banks, this long corridor has considerable strategic value, for it gives European ships fishing outside the Canadian zone access to a port in North America without having to submit to any Canadian controls. The expansions at the Inter-Pêche plant in Saint-Pierre by its new Spanish owners, at a cost of ten million dollars, bears witness to the role that was planned for it.

It is very likely that if Saint-Pierre residents do not obtain from Canada the groundfish quotas that they feel are due to them by virtue of the reaffirmation of the 1972 Franco-Canadian agreements contained in the New York tribunal's decision,* they will seek to take the fish outside the Canadian zone. In fact, Canada's proposed quotas are only roughly one-tenth the expectations of Saint-Pierre residents. If a good fishing day provides a catch of some fifty tonnes of fish, this would mean fewer than ten days of fishing per year for each of the seven trawlers in the French archipelago.

But where will anyone find these fish? There are obviously hardly enough cod to satisfy the needs of Saint-Pierre and Miquelon in the Gulf; the allocations, some forty-five hundred tonnes in 1992, have been cut by 60 per cent for Canadians for 1993. The inshore fishermen, for their part, advocate a moratorium in the Gulf similar to that in the Grand Banks, and some even say that it should last five years instead of eighteen months! Thus, all of eastern Canada faces a deep crisis.

Nor can France be offered groundfish quotas in southern Nova Scotia: all commercial species are being exploited to their maximum sustainable yield, and even beyond it. It is the domino effect produced when a particular stock collapses: the fishing effort shifts to the other stocks and ends up

---

* These agreements, made before the redfish stocks in the Gulf of St. Lawrence collapsed, required Canada to grant to the fresh-fish trawlers of Saint-Pierre and Miquelon groundfish quotas "corresponding to their needs", because of France's historical fishing rights in the Gulf.

threatening them all in their turn. This was what had happened after the first cod crisis, in 1968, when the trawlers were compensated with redfish quotas: in five years the stock was decimated by the large trawlers. Canada then allocated to the plunderers excessive quotas in the cod stocks, which were just beginning to recover, with results that are now only too well known.

Today, we are again foundering in past errors. Reshuffling the allocations between fishing fleets is proving to be a gargantuan task, for which the Department of Fisheries has not come forward with a solution as of this writing. Some cod fisherman may be compensated with redfish quotas—but at what risk to the redfish? To compensate for the effect on the Newfoundland offshore fleet of the moratorium on northern cod, the Canadian government has increased the catch quota for turbot (Greenland halibut) by twenty thousand tonnes. Addressing a meeting in St. Anthony, in northern Newfoundland, an inshore fisherman declared that there weren't enough turbot in the sea to provide supper for everyone in the room!

Obviously, we are still not preparing a rosy future for ourselves.

For although the biometricists and other Canadian fishery managers still conclude, with their numbers to support them, that this inshore fisherman is a crank who speaks through his hat, their performance over the years has been less than impressive. Never have the fisheries been in poorer condition than since Fisheries and Oceans Canada has exercised exclusive control over them. It must be said, in all fairness, that the groundfisheries were already doing poorly. But it is also true that a lesson could have been learned from past errors and applied to improve management in the future, although this hasn't been the case.

On the contrary, we have apparently not learned a thing. It seems that the fishery simply cannot be managed at a long-term sustainable yield. The proof of this is the terrible situation that prevails in the fishery of species that were little or not at all exploited before Fisheries and Oceans Canada imposed itself as the sole manager of all fishery activities, in-shore and offshore: snow crab and shrimp.

In 1975, snow crabs were still called *chancre* by Acadian fishermen and thrown back into the sea because there was no market for them. Their rapid rise in popularity was due, among other things, to their formidable abundance because they had never been fished and to the collapse of Alaska crab stocks on the Pacific coast. The Japanese, the principal con-sumers of snow crabs, were looking for new supply sources. When exploratory fisheries by New Brunswick fishermen (Caraquet, Shippegan) proved more than satisfactory, ex-ploitation of the resource developed rapidly. Soon, old Gaspé codfishing ships, then some from the Magdalen Islands, also obtained permits, and they all had fabulous fishing for several years. In two months of work, the deck hands earned thirty or forty thousand dollars, and sometimes more.

To share the abundance more equitably, and relieve the pressure on other species, especially cod, Fisheries and Oceans Canada handed out more snow-crab permits. Then, even when the overall catches began to drop, in the second half of the 1980s, it granted further permits, this time to Prince Edward Island fishermen, in the name of equal access to the resources (even declining ones) by all provinces. Final-ly, there were too many permits and the catches really began to tumble. In the meantime, landing prices dropped because of over-production and an increase in Alaska crab catches in the Pacific. In the end, crab fishing, which had made the first who ventured into it prosperous (those who had researched and developed it) no longer provides a decent living for any fisherman, and the resource is in a lamentable state of deple-tion.

The story of fishing for shrimp, scallops, and lumpfish (for the roe) follows roughly the same curve: abundance of the virgin resource, prosperity of the first fishermen, emission of too many permits, drop in prices and collapse of the resource, and finally, difficulty for anyone to make a living with it. People note, bitter-ly, that the bureaucrats responsible for this poor management keep their jobs until they retire, while their "resource," human beings, are shuffled from Fisheries and Oceans to Employment (read unemployment) Canada, then to Social Affairs, thus providing lots of work for still other bureaucrats.

I will return to discuss the pernicious effects on the fishery of a public service that, like everyone, looks after its own priorities to begin with. But I do want to point out that fishery management is not uniformly bad, as one might think from all of the above. There are in fact certain species that are well managed: not only are catches maintained over the years, but the resource even grows continually.

The paradigm is lobster, and the paradigm of paradigms is lobster in the Magdalen Islands, where I've been living and observing the fisheries for twenty years. Here, lobster catches have grown year to year, from an average of a thousand tonnes in 1969 through 1972 to an average of 2,500 tonnes from 1989 to 1992.

How can this be explained? First, and most obviously, the resource tolerates it—or has tolerated it up to now, because there will inevitably be a ceiling to its growth. This tolerance is due to adequate protection measures: a two-month fishing season every year; access to the fishery limited to an almost constant number of ships, each with a finite number of traps (three hundred); the requirement to discard lobsters that have not reached a certain size as well as berried females; and dissuasive sanctions against infractions and poaching. It must also be mentioned that management of lobsters is made easier by the fact that it is an almost sedentary species, which moves only moderately within a well-defined perimeter.

There was fear, some years ago, that the increase in catches was resulting from the use of more sophisticated catching gear. Ten years before, fishermen used a compass, an echo sounder, and their reading of the sea—the experience passed down from generation to generation—to tend their traps in the rocky lobster grounds. Now, all the ships are equipped with navigation instruments that locate lobster grounds extremely accurately. As well, the new ships are more seaworthy, capable of navigating in seas once almost or completely unmanageable, which increases significantly the number of

fishing days per season. Some fishermen worry that the combination of these two factors will result in a decline, or even a
collapse, of the resource in a few seasons. However, the
record catches this year seem to contradict their fears.

The explanation, according to some, relates to the decrease in
populations of cod and plaice, which are major predators of lobster larvae during the spawning season. It remains to evaluate the
impact of the use of "jumbo" traps, almost twice as big as the
traditional ones, on catches and the resource. Will there be a
sudden fall in catches after another record year because all the
lobster will have been caught, or will the fishery stabilize at its
maximum sustainable yield over the long term?

Whatever the reason, the lobster fishery has done well up
to the present, and there is no doubt that at the first sign of
failure, appropriate measures will be taken to correct the
situation. And these will be respected by all fishermen, for
the excellent reason that they are inshore, local fishermen,
who feel that they collectively own their resource, who have
an atavistic and willful attachment to what they perceive as
their exclusive property.

It would be very poorly received indeed if the government decided to palliate a hypothetical lack of lobster in, say, Shédiac by
transferring a certain number of permits to the Magdalen Islands or the Bay of Gaspé. In fact, such a measure is utterly unthinkable! However, this is what constantly happens with
groundfish management: zones are opened or closed to trawlers
from everywhere. They are distributed, shared, and dispersed so
much that no offshore fisherman considers the resource his or
feels very involved in its protection. Shunted from one fishery to
another, as the fish get rarer and rarer, he seeks above all to get
something out of it for himself. And although he is consulted
through his associations, and invited to sit on committees with
other fishermen, company owners, and government representatives, he knows that the divergence of interests is such that
differences are ultimately settled in favour of those who hold power; as well-intentioned as they may, these exercises in consultation are often nothing but simulacra. In fact, there are no
miracles to be made: there are no more fish.

And the incontestable corollary of this desolating reality is
that there are too many fishermen: for the last half-dozen
years, the government has been trying to reduce their numbers. Sea workers who receive government aid the most readi-
ly, are those who decide to get out of the trade, retrain for
another job, and move to a region where employment is less
rare than beside the sea. Thus they become eligible for sub-
sidies through various programmes with euphemistic names,
such as the Northern Cod Adjustment and Recovery Program
and the Federal Programme for Fisheries Development in
Québec (a misleading name if there ever was one!), which are
administered by Fisheries and Oceans Canada.

The law imposing an eighteen-month moratorium on
northern cod fishing in Newfoundland also has provisions for
fishermen to sell their boats and gear and learn a new skill.
Without shouting it from the rooftops, the government hopes
that the effects of forced unemployment in the small fishing
communities will be to incite people to look for work elsewhere. The small inshore fishermen who have not yet
thrown in the towel believe that the aim of the policy is
simply to eliminate them.

Meanwhile, although one is led to believe the contrary, fishing continues on Newfoundland's Grand Banks. Only the cod
fishery is closed, which necessarily affects other fisheries,
such as flatfish, in which cod represents a high percentage of
bycatches. To attenuate the effect of the moratorium on codfishing, for which the annual quota for Canadian vessels had
been around 120,000 tonnes, the government has authorized
the taking of 20,000 additional tonnes of turbot. There are
thus Canadian ships fishing turbot, pollock, redfish, and so
on. But there are also a some foreign vessels catching
"surplus" species—that is, those whose numbers are
presumed to be in excess of our needs: mackerel, capelin,
squid, tuna, grenadier, and so on.

It is very difficult to obtain accurate information on how
many permits Canada hands out to foreign ships for harvesting surplus species. Only a few M.P.s, who felt that it was

their responsibility as representatives of the people, have managed to penetrate this arcana, although they haven't always received all of the information they asked for.

One M.P. has learned that Japan, which once had seventeen unlimited tuna-fishing permits in Canadian waters, has had its fleet reduced to seven ships, but they are double the size, which means that their total catching power has not changed much. The Tuna Management Commission, which comprises Japan, the United States, and Canada, imposes quotas only on bluefin, the most popular tuna variety. These quotas are divided as follows in Canadian waters: Japan, 1,350 tonnes; the United States, 750 tonnes; Canada, 570 tonnes. As for other tuna varieties (albacore, big eye, yellowfin, skipjack), Japan can still fish them in unlimited quantities.

Canada also offers a large number of mackerel-fishing permits to foreign vessels, notably Polish and Bulgarian ones. They can fish starting in June, before the spawning season, and can range into the interior of the Gulf of St. Lawrence. They thus intercept not only the mackerel schools in their seasonal migration, but also herring, and their take of the latter amounts to 30 per cent of their take of the former. These ships also have catch quotas equivalent to unlimited quantities. The only restriction that appears on the permits granted to the Bulgarians is that for each five thousand tonnes of mackerel fished by their ships, one thousand tonnes must be purchased from or processed by Canadians. The Polish, according to information I have obtained, can catch as much mackerel as they want.

Since mackerel, especially when small, are prey for the cod, such catch permits must have some kind of impact on the growth of cod stocks. Besides, to give out unlimited fishing permits before the spawning season also bears witness to an aberrant temerity on the part of the Canadian managers. A mackerel in fact grows to the phenomenal size of 20 cm in its first three months of growth, which means that the biomass of the schools is much greater in the fall than in the spring. As well, in some years there is a mysterious phenomenon of mortality among the adults due to causes other than fishing,* which can affect up to 20 per cent of the schools.

If permits to foreign vessels were restricted to late summer and early fall, the mackerel would be fished after they have reproduced and before they die of natural causes—which is the very art of fishing—and the cod would have more smaller individuals to eat, and Canadian inshore fishermen would have more "small mackerel" with which to bait their lobster traps the following spring. Tuna, which feed on mackerel during their autumn migration southward, demonstrate better ecological sense in this regard than *homo industrialis!*

Another species that is fished in unlimited quantities by foreign ships in Canadian waters is squid. Until the 1960s, they were caught within the Gulf of St. Lawrence, up to Percé. They were not very popular as food, with their tentacles, their viscous aspect, and their ugliness; but they were used as bait, since they are a favourite food of cod.

Squid live only one year, during which they migrate from the shores of Florida to the Grand Banks of Canada and back. It is thus essential for the survival of the species that a sufficient number of individuals complete the entire migratory cycle. Aerial photos of the migration, which once revealed a large, dense black river flowing parallel to the coast, now show only a narrow rivulet.

This does not keep Canada from continuing to allocate unlimited catch permits for squid to foreign ships, even in the zone where cod depend largely on them for food—and where capelin, mackerel, and herring are already the object of generous quotas given to foreign fleets.

"It's not very suprising," the M.P. from whom I got most of this information told me, "that the cod are growing more slowly in certain regions of our fishing banks, since we take away everything they eat!"

---

* Biologists attribute this to sudden cooling of the water.

As well as fishing permits for "surplus" species, Fisheries and Oceans Canada also gives foreign vessels "scientific" and "experimental" permits valid in Canada's exclusive economic zone. According to many, these licensed ships, like all the others, take bycatches of cod equivalent to those of a directed fishery. But the terms of the contracts to which these licenses are subjected do not even provide for Canadian observers on board these vessels. And there are quite a few! In fact, Canada has granted, for better or for worse, fifteen experimental and thirty research permits to foreigners without even giving itself the right to see what's going on. This means a total of forty-five ships, all of them fifty-five metres long and more. There are only two ships of this size in the entire Canadian fishing fleet!

Now, as a result of the so-called historic agreement with the European Community signed on 21 December 1992, a one-year deal whose value is mainly symbolic and which can be rejected by either party on six weeks' notice, the Europeans will also be granted access to our "surplus species" in our own E.E.Z., along with other NAFO partners.

Aside from the fact that Fisheries and Oceans Canada displays incredible laxness in collecting fees for the fishing, research, and experimental licenses it hands out to foreign ships (some are behind by two years!)—it certainly gives no such latitude to Canadian fishermen—the paperwork for so many foreign ships in Canada's two-hundred-mile zone must occupy numerous civil servants. I have been told that up to a third of the Oceans and Fisheries Canada staff in Halifax spend their time on one aspect or another of the international fishery, and there are more in St. John's and Ottawa. In short, the work of a significant portion of the department is justified by the management of the foreign fishery.

One reason it is not easy to get rid of foreigners in our fishing zone, my M.P. source told me, is that too many bureaucrats have a direct interest in having them keep on fishing. Like everyone, in these recessionary times, they want to protect their jobs.

Refusing to let himself be beaten by the moratorium on cod-fishing, this summer a Newfoundland fisherman from the Avalon Peninsula, south of St. John's, equipped his small fifty-five-foot (eighteen-metre) trawler to fish turbot in the northern waters a hundred and fifty miles from the coast. There, on the high seas, there were a few other ships, some Canadian, but mostly foreign vessels three, four, and even five times larger than his, which were fishing "surplus" species and taking at the same time not negligible cod bycatches. Never mind: the small Newfoundland fisher shot out his nets and trawled. He caught turbot and also cod, which the rules required him to discard once he had taken his limit of 10 per cent bycatch.

He had been fishing for a day or two when he saw on the horizon the silhouette of a Canadian patrol boat. Well, he thought, at least the government is conducting surveillance. But to his great surprise, the ship came straight toward him, although he was surrounded by the giant ships of the foreign fleets, and in fact boarded him first.

They inspected his gear, his ship log, his catch report, and his hold. After a few hours, everything was found to be legal and in order, and the inspectors returned to their ship, which sailed off. With his binoculars, the Newfoundland fisherman watched it draw away. He saw it tack a few times among the huge trawlers of the foreign fleet, then turn around and disappear over the horizon, without having boarded one. His ship, the smallest, and Canadian to boot, fishing in his own territorial waters, had been the sole object of their surveillance. He was still very upset when he returned to port, all the more so because an ocean storm had forced him to come in while the others could ride it out at sea.

Epilogue

NOW IT IS SEPTEMBER, and the autumn winds are already ruf-
fling the sea into whitecaps. In Makkovik, where there was
no fishing, the first squalls of snow and hail are already brew-
ing, warning of the coming winter. It was the time when
once, after the cod had been dried on the beaches and flakes
and sold to the merchants in the south, the men would have
gone out to the forest to cut their firewood. This year, 1992,
for the first time in at least 450 years, no cod dried in the sun
on the flakes of Newfoundland's east coast. Some people call
this progress.

Newfoundlander friends have told me that the fishermen
on forced unemployment insurance are taking their bad luck
philosophically, anaesthetized by their small subsistence che-
que and the reassuring words of the Canadian government.
Some actually believe the official propaganda that tells them
that in fifteen months the cod will be back, just like in the
good old days!

In the Gaspé, in order not to lose the Italian market for the
famous Gaspé Cure dried salt cod, they have had to import
frozen Pacific cod from Alaska. Transported by boat to Vancouver, then by truck to its destination, it travels a total of six
thousand kilometres before being laid out in the Gaspé sun
on the long slatted tables called *vigneaux*, which cover entire
fields in the counterforts of the Chic-Choc Mountains.

In the Magdalen Islands, like everywhere in the Gulf of St.
Lawrence, summer brought poor fishing for the inshore
fishermen. They returned to port at the end of the afternoon,
after twelve hours out at sea, with one or two petty basketfuls
of fish. Not even a hundred kilos! I watched crates being
hoisted onto the dock, and I read on the fishermen' faces not
just immense weariness and sadness, but also a sort of
shame, as if they felt diminished by doing their job with so
little reward or somehow guilty for the lack of fish. And I
remembered when, ten years earlier, in times which, according to them, were not even as plentiful as before, they rolled

up their sleeves and hoisted from their hold fourteen, fifteen, sixteen crates of plump cod and grey plaice, exchanging jokes with the weigher up on the wharf.

At Millerand, one of the main landing ports for Magdalen Islands inshore fishermen, one-tonne crates, which once would not have been large enough to hold the catch from a single boat, could now hold the catch from five or six. It consisted of very small cod, maybe a forearm long, mixed with a few plaice—not the nice grey flatfish, a fine variety, that were caught before, but ordinary yellow-tail, which were once used as lobster bait.

Wellie Lebel, who has fished cod and plaice all his life, was with me. For every ship that came in, he told me what kind of gear they were fishing with: this one, long lines; that one, nets; over there, jiggers. But they all had the same disappointing catches.

"It's the Danish seines that killed the fishery for the small inshore fishermen," he said, in his musical Acadian French. "Since they started, we don't see any more plaice. Before, all through late July and early August, it was plaice! The fishery ought to be closed in the Gulf for at least five years to give the fish a chance to come back. At least five years! If not, it's over."

And he picked up a small cod, with a sort of affectionate tenderness. "Before, we didn't keep these; we threw them back. The plant didn't take them. But now, it takes everything. They even fillet tiny things like this!"

To provide relief to the inshore fishermen, whose meagre catches didn't even cover their expenses, the government has offered them a salary supplement to experiment with new, more selective gear. But how long will this palliative care last if the fish stocks don't recover?

In the meantime, as Canadian fishermen were idled by the northern cod moratorium or fishing other cod populations or other endangered species (the Greenland halibut), the NAFO meeting that ended on 18 September 1992 at Dartmouth, Nova Scotia, did not bring cheerful prospects for those who know how to read marine charts. The EC countries had agreed to prolong their moratorium on fishing in the 3L management zone. This was almost as symbolic a concession as the one they had made in June 1992, announcing that they were pulling back their fleets from the 2J3KL zones for six months, when they knew very well that the northern cod migrated to the coasts at this time.

If one examines the NAFO management map, one sees that only a quarter of the 3L zone is situated outside Canada's E.E.Z., including, it is true, the Nose of the Grand Banks. In fact, all that the EC is giving up is a band of some 50,000 square kilometres of ocean. It has not agreed to reduce its cod quotas in zone 3M, immediately east of 3L, which covers the gently descending continental slope and the Flemish Cap. Since the cod winter in these depths, between two and six hundred metres, there is much northern cod in zone 3M, the same northern cod for which there is a moratorium on fishing, as we know, for Newfoundland fishermen. Moreover, the EC can fish the independent Flemish Cap stock to its content.

It is difficult to understand, under these circumstances, the satisfaction expressed by the Canadian minister of fisheries and oceans, John Crosbie, at the end of this NAFO meeting. "Canada has attained its objective," he declared in *The Sou'-Wester*, the fisheries industry journal. "The organization u-nanimously supports the moratorium on fishing northern cod outside Canada's two-hundred-mile territorial waters."

I beg to be skeptical. The European concession appears to me to be purely symbolic. They are pulling back seventy-five kilometres to the east and no more. If Canada's victory had truly been so stunning, we would no doubt have heard of it in the national press, especially because the proponents of one of the two options for the referendum on the Charlottetown Accord, to be held in October of 1992, desperately needed this type of good news to boost their cause. But neither the NAFO meeting nor the minister's comments made headlines on the television news or in the major newspapers. Only the local press reported it, and without much critical analysis.

What's more, countries that are not NAFO members, the "flags of convenience"—Panama, South Korea, and the like—are not included in the moratorium in the 50,000 square kilometres of zone 3L, because they are not NAFO signatories. They currently represent about 15 per cent of the ships and of the catch of the fleets fishing at the limit of the Canadian E.E.Z. Nothing, except concerted diplomatic pressure by the fishing countries, will persuade them to abandon zone 3L. And it is strongly suspected that some European fishing enterprises supply their plants with the catch from these ships.

The demand for cod in Portugal and Spain will remain strong, whether there is much or almost none left in the ocean. In the food markets of Santiago de Compostela, in the windows of the fish stores in Porto, in front of the Dos Clerigos tower, there will always be heaps of dried cod, sorted by size and selling at between eight and twelve dollars a kilo, a little more for the *"Bacalhau de Norvega"*; in Portuguese restaurants, they will always serve salads of potatoes, onions, cod, and olive oil, the national dish. The British will not give up their fish and chips made with baby cod, nor will the processing plants in Scotland stop manufacturing them, unless a vigorous campaign makes them aware of the ecological catastrophe in which they are accomplices. And even if they reform their eating habits, stop the commerce in juvenile fish, and so on, the payments on the modern, high-performance Portuguese and Spanish trawlers will still have to be made.

On the other hand, the Saint-Pierre question has to be considered. Since Canada has refused France the groundfish quotas it requested, tension has risen between Newfoundland and Saint-Pierre–Miquelon. As a retaliatory measure, France has ejected from its twenty-five-mile exclusive zone around the archipelago Newfoundlanders who had been fishing scallops there for twenty years. Two more plants on the Rock are threatened with closure.

This aggravated situation leaves the vague plans mentioned at the end of May by Mr. Beaufils (Franco-Canadian cooperation in surveillance and policing of fisheries in the seas off Canada) wilting on the vine. As for the groundfish that Canada is denying Saint-Pierre, it is very likely that they will look for it elsewhere, since it is a question of life and death for the French archipelago. We will then see how useful the two-hundred-mile umbilical cord linking Saint-Pierre and Miquelon to international waters will prove.

In desperation, a group of Canadian fisheries company owners and union leaders, calling themselves SONAR (Save Our Northwest Atlantic Resource), appealed to the United Nations to intervene and temporarily accord exclusive management of the Grand Banks cod to Canada until it implemented an effective management system for the fish in the high seas. People in this group called NAFO a paper tiger.

Their goal would not be an easy one to reach. First, the other fishing countries would have to cooperate and then find a way to respect this agreement; and who would pay the bill, given the disastrous state of the United Nations' finances? Nevertheless, the Canadian industry itself, with this cry for help, seems to hope that the United Nations will intervene again in the northwest Atlantic fishing zones (ICNAF was a United Nations agency). This seems to indicate that, in their eyes, Canadian policy has failed and the nationalism of the 1980s with regard to fisheries management is dead.[*] Meanwhile, Canada has convened in early 1993 a meeting of some 57 coastal nations to discuss this question. Internationalism is in the air.

At a time when talk of globalization of markets and economies is all the rage, and when an entire continent is dying of hunger, an international agency such as the FAO would perhaps be the most appropriate to take up world management of the fisheries. Its first act would have to ensure the long-term sustainable yield of the fish stocks, not only to satisfy the nutritional needs of an exponentially ex-

---

[*] One of the items in the December 21, 1992 accord between Canada and the European Community calls for an international Law of the Sea conference to be convened in New York in June of 1993.

panding world population, but also, as a corollary, to ensure a future for the fisheries industry, which is in the process of blindly sawing off the branch on which it is sitting.

But it is also possible that the dilemma of the fisheries in the northwest Atlantic is not as simple as re-establishing an equilibrium between catches and resources. A growing number of scientists think that pollution of the oceans and climatic conditions, such as the cooling of waters mentioned recently by the highest scientific authorities in the Canadian fisheries, will slow the pace of the regeneration of wild stocks, and notably those of cod.

In this case, the only thing left to do—and fast—would be to allocate more resources to fish farming. Great strides have been made in this area over the last twenty or thirty years; tens of thousands of tonnes of fish, shellfish, and mollusks are currently produced through farming, either in the open sea or in land-based pools. FAO experts (again) agree that water is the ideal medium for producing foods. Indeed, while a hectare of good pastureland can produce several hundred kilos of meat, the same area of water can supply two tonnes and more of fish and a hundred tonnes of shellfish.

Fish farming is already responsible for a good part of world production of certain mollusks and shelfish, while salmon and trout (or char) raised in pens in the sea supply a good part of the market for these fine species on both sides of the Atlantic. The deep fjords of Norway, awash in temperate and fertile Gulf Stream waters, are such breeding pools, producing a sole comparable to that of Dover and a miniature halibut that reaches a weight of seven kilograms in three years.

In Canada, water temperature and ice forestall such results. In many places, the breeding fish must be transferred from sea enclosures in the summer to land-based pools fed with briny water in the winter. But, in spite of these handicaps and several years' lag in such large producing countries as Japan, Iceland, Norway, Sweden, Spain, and others, the results seem to augur well for the future.

At the *Institut Maurice Lamontagne* in Sainte-Flavie, Québec, and in Bay Bulls, Newfoundland, researchers are raising cod, which is a relatively recent and promising technique. The cod grow rapidly in salty and slightly briny water, sometimes doubling in weight from one to two kilograms in two months, thanks to a food/weight conversion rate of three to one in fish-farming conditions, compared to ten to one in natural conditions. The fish used are those of small size culled from the fishery. Artificial fertilization of the eggs remains technically very difficult to accomplish. The biological aspect of this technology seems however to be sufficiently developed that at present research will be pursued in a semi-industrial context.

In some countries, according to a recent article in the journal *France-Pêche*, other types of experiments with farming fish in their natural environment have been conducted. Some kinds of fish, released into the water near the coasts, get into the habit of coming back to their point of departure to receive their food, just like herds of cattle let loose on the prairie will return to the barn in the evening all by themselves.

This is certainly an exaltant poetic vision!

But by the time the small inshore fisherman becomes the shepherd of the fish schools, and notably of the cod, as successful as he once was when his nets were full of cod "as big as a man", his traditional way of life may be only an anachronism, a curiosity portrayed in museums on the Atlantic coast of Canada, killed off by a gigantic, counter-productive industry. From which country hardly matters.

Pointe-Basse
June–December 1992

Table of Contents